Introduction

Like the wonderful variety and diversity of the p[eople] we know and love, this afghan collection offers designs as varied as our homes and decorating [styles]. Our impressive collection of 47 cozy crochet afghans—in many different styles, textures and co[lor] combinations—offers innovative ideas for every home. We've used a variety of the beautiful yarns that are readily available to us from our favorite major yarn companies.

You'll find warm, densely crocheted cover-ups for the coldest of weather, lovely lacy designs for elegant accessorizing, fresh floral and fruit motifs to use as fun accents and colorful variations to brighten a friend in the doldrums. You can even prepare for the next baby shower with clever new designs to comfort a newborn or toddler at naptime.

Our stitching reference guide with easy-to-follow illustrations will make it a snap for both beginner crocheters or infrequent crocheters to delve into this relaxing needlecraft with few snags. So while you are paging through all the exciting full-color photographs and think you would like to make afghans as appealing as these, be assured that everything you need to know to insure your success is included in this book.

Contents

Stripes & Strips 5

Alpine Memories 6
Cheer Up 9
Diagonal Hues 13
I Love Scraps 16
Mountain Trails 19
Shady Glen 22
Spring Waves 25
Themes and Variations 28
Color Me Happy 30

Garden Florals 33

Blanket of Peonies 34
Castle Grounds 38
Day Lilies 43
Parlor Bouquet 47
Rose Dreams 50
Wedding Roses 53
Wearing of the Green 56

Out of the Ordinary 59

A Little Bit of Chocolate 60
Antique Lace 63
Baltic Tiles 66
Blue Lagoon 69
Flower Power 72
Lollipop Confection 75
Old Cathedral 79
Simply Scrumptious 82

City Sophistication 85

Autumn Afternoon 86
City Escape 89
Impressionist Ripple 91
Night and Day 94
Ombré for Your Hombré 97
Pavé Diamonds 99
Sonata 102
Spanish Tiles 107
Twilight Tapestry 110

Country 113

Christmas Floral 114
Diagonal Diamonds 118
Harmony 120
Remember the Kittens 123
Pinwheel Roses 125
Rainbow's End 128
Strawberry Jam 131
Watermelon Picnic 135

Especially for Baby 139

Angel Clouds 140
Grandma's Pride 143
Merry-Go-Rounds 146
My Little Sunshine 150
Pretty Peppermint 153
Ruffles for Baby 156

General Information

Abbreviations & Symbols .. 158
Word About Gauge 158
Filet Review 159
Fringe 159
Stitch Guide 160
Metric Charts 160

Stripes & Strips

*I*f you're looking for colorful drama and lively colorations, here's a selection of afghans you'll love. You'll find ripples and zigzags, side to side styles, horizontal and vertical and diagonal stripes and even this design to use up your scraps with rows of hearts.

Alpine Memories	6
Cheer Up	9
Diagonal Hues	13
I Love Scraps	16
Mountain Trails	19
Shady Glen	22
Spring Waves	25
Themes and Variations	28
Color Me Happy	30

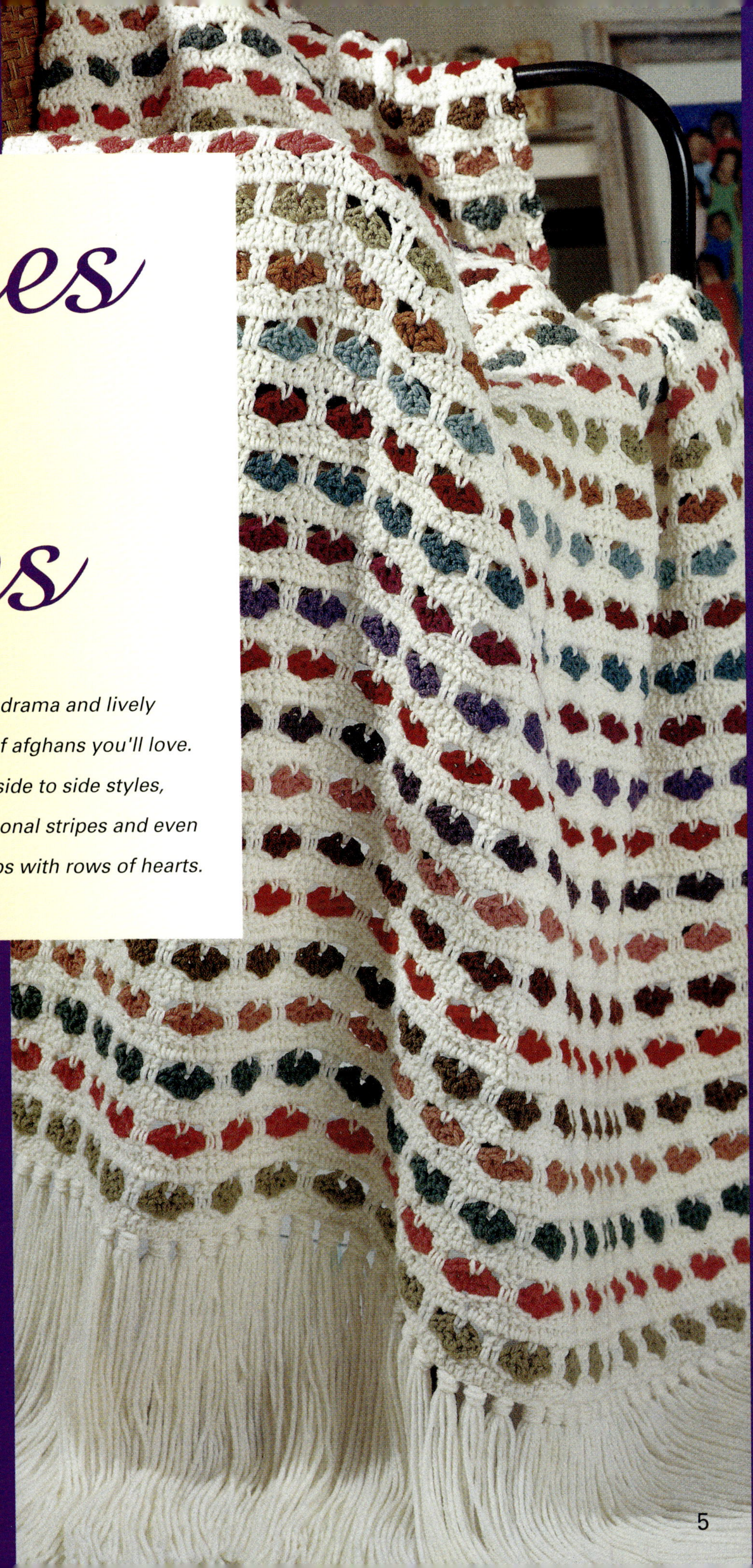

Alpine Memories
designed by Denise Black

The zigzag of the ripple pattern is reminiscent of mountain scenery. A great choice for beginner crocheters, this design can be made in any favorite color scheme.

Size:
About 45" x 60"

Materials:
Worsted weight yarn, 15 oz (1050 yds, 450 gms) each, burgundy and green; 16 oz (1120 yds, 480 gms) flecked yarn

Note: *Our photographed afghan was made with Red Heart® Super Saver, Dark Sage #633, and Cranberry #7760; Red Heart® Fiesta, Soft White #6316.*

Size H (5mm) crochet hook, or size required for gauge
Size 16 tapestry needle

Gauge:
4 dc = 1"

Pattern Stitch

Cluster (CL):
Keeping last lp of each dc on hook, dc in 2 sts indicated, YO and draw through all 3 lps on hook—CL made.

Instructions

Note: *To change color, work until 2 lps of last st remain on hook. With new color, YO and draw through 2 lps on hook. Cut old color.*

With green, ch 211.

Row 1 (right side):
Dc in 3rd ch from hook (beg 2 skipped chs count as a dc) and in next 3 chs; [CL (see Pattern Stitch) over next 2 chs] 3 times; dc in next 3 chs; * 3 dc in next ch; dc in next 3 chs, (CL over next 2 chs) 3 times; dc in next 3 chs; rep from * 14 times more; 2 dc in last ch, changing to tweed in last dc. Ch 2 (counts as first dc on following rows), turn.

Row 2:
2 dc in first dc; ch 2, sk next 3 dc, sc in next dc, ch 4, sk next 3 dc, sc in next dc, ch 2; * sk next 3 dc, 5 dc in next dc; ch 2, sk next 3 dc, sc in next dc, ch 4, sk next 3 dc, sc in next dc, ch 2; rep from * to last 3 dc and beg 2 skipped chs; sk last 3 dc, 3 dc in 2nd ch of beg 2 skipped chs. Ch 2, turn.

Row 3:
Dc in first dc, 2 dc in next dc; dc in next dc, ch 2, sk next ch-2 sp, sc in next ch-4 sp, ch 2, sk next sc, dc in next dc, 2 dc in next dc; * 3 dc in next dc; 2 dc in next dc; dc in next dc, ch 2, sk next ch-2 sp, sc in next ch-4 sp, ch 2, sk next sc, dc in next dc, 2 dc in next dc; rep from * to turning ch; 2 dc in 2nd ch of turning ch-2, changing to burgundy. Ch 2, turn.

continued

Alpine Memories

Row 4:
Sk first dc, (2 dc in next dc, dc in next dc) twice; sk next sc, dc in next dc; * (2 dc in next dc, dc in next dc) 4 times; sk next sc, dc in next dc; rep from * to last 3 dc and turning ch; 2 dc in next dc; dc in next dc, 2 dc in next dc; dc in 2nd ch of turning ch-2. Ch 2, turn.

Row 5:
Dc in first 4 dc, (CL over next 2 dc) 3 times; dc in next 3 dc; * 3 dc in next dc; dc in next 3 dc, (CL over next 2 dc) 3 times; dc in next 3 dc; rep from * to turning ch; 2 dc in 2nd ch of turning ch-2, changing to green. Ch 2, turn.

Row 6:
2 dc in first dc; ch 2, sk next 3 dc, sc in next dc, ch 4, sk next 3 dc, sc in next dc, ch 2; * sk next 3 dc, 5 dc in next dc; ch 2, sk next 3 dc, sc in next dc, ch 4, sk next 3 dc, sc in next dc, ch 2; rep from * to last 3 dc and turning ch; sk next 3 dc, 3 dc in 2nd ch of turning ch-2. Ch 2, turn.

Row 7:
Dc in first dc, 2 dc in next dc; dc in next dc, ch 2, sk next ch-2 sp, sc in next ch-4 sp, ch 2, sk next sc, dc in next dc, 2 dc in next dc; * 3 dc in next dc; 2 dc in next dc; dc in next dc, ch 2, sk next ch-2 sp, sc in next ch-4 sp, ch 2, sk next sc, dc in next dc, 2 dc in next dc; rep from * to turning ch; 2 dc in 2nd ch of turning ch-2, changing to flecked yarn. Ch 2, turn.

Row 8:
Sk first dc, (2 dc in next dc, dc in next dc) twice; sk next sc, dc in next dc; * (2 dc in next dc, dc in next dc) 4 times; sk next sc, dc in next dc; rep from * to last 3 dc and turning ch; 2 dc in next dc; dc in next dc, 2 dc in next dc; dc in 2nd ch of turning ch-2. Ch 2, turn.

Row 9:
Dc in first 4 dc, (CL over next 2 dc) 3 times; dc in next 3 dc; * 3 dc in next dc; dc in next 3 dc, (CL over next 2 dc) 3 times; dc in next 3 dc; rep from * to turning ch; 2 dc in 2nd ch of turning ch-2, changing to burgundy. Ch 2, turn.

Row 10:
2 dc in first dc; ch 2, sk next 3 dc, sc in next dc, ch 4, sk next 3 dc, sc in next dc, ch 2; * sk next 3 dc, 5 dc in next dc; ch 2, sk next 3 dc, sc in next dc, ch 4, sk next 3 dc, sc in next dc, ch 2; rep from * to last 3 dc and turning ch; sk next 3 dc, 3 dc in 2nd ch of turning ch-2. Ch 2, turn.

Row 11:
Dc in first dc, 2 dc in next dc; dc in next dc, ch 2, sk next ch-2 sp, sc in next ch-4 sp, ch 2, sk next sc, dc in next dc, 2 dc in next dc; * 3 dc in next dc; 2 dc in next dc; dc in next dc, ch 2, sk next ch-2 sp, sc in next ch-4 sp, ch 2, sk next sc, dc in next dc, 2 dc in next dc; rep from * to turning ch; 2 dc in 2nd ch of turning ch-2, changing to green. Ch 2, turn.

Row 12:
Sk first dc, (2 dc in next dc, dc in next dc) twice; sk next sc, dc in next dc; * (2 dc in next dc, dc in next dc) 4 times; sk next sc, dc in next dc; rep from * to last 3 dc and turning ch; 2 dc in next dc; dc in next dc, 2 dc in next dc; dc in 2nd ch of turning ch-2. Ch 2, turn.

Row 13:
Dc in first 4 dc, (CL over next 2 dc) 3 times; dc in next 3 dc; * 3 dc in next dc; dc in next 3 dc, (CL over next 2 dc) 3 times; dc in next 3 dc; rep from * to turning ch; 2 dc in 2nd ch of turning ch-2, changing to flecked yarn. Ch 2, turn.

Row 14:
2 dc in first dc; ch 2, sk next 3 dc, sc in next dc, ch 4, sk next 3 dc, sc in next dc, ch 2; * sk next 3 dc, 5 dc in next dc; ch 2, sk next 3 dc, sc in next dc, ch 4, sk next 3 dc, sc in next dc, ch 2; rep from * to last 3 dc and turning ch; sk next 3 dc, 3 dc in 2nd ch of turning ch-2. Ch 2, turn.

Rep Rows 3 through 14 until piece measures about 60", ending with a Row 4. At end of last row, do not ch 2.

Finish off and weave in all ends.

Cheer Up designed by Eleanor Albano-Miles

Using a colorful variegated yarn, the bobble clusters in these strips and squares are great fun to crochet. This cheery afghan is the perfect gift for someone who needs cheering up.

Cheer Up

Size:
About 43" x 58" before fringe

Materials:
Worsted weight yarn, 33 oz (2310 yds, 990 gms) variegated; 30 oz (2100 yds, 900 gms) blue

Note: Our photographed afghan was made with Red Heart® Soft, Seascape #962 and Skipper Blue #384.

Size J (6mm) crochet hook, or size required for gauge
Size 16 tapestry needle

Gauge:
7 sc = 2"

Pattern Stitch

Cluster (CL):
Keeping last lp of each dc on hook, 4 dc in st indicated, YO and draw through all 5 lps on hook; ch 1—CL made.

Instructions

Motif (make 27)
With variegated, ch 16.

Row 1 (wrong side):
Sc in 2nd ch from hook and in each rem ch—15 sc. Ch 1, turn.

Row 2 (right side):
Sc in first sc, CL (see Pattern Stitch) in next sc; sc in next sc; * CL in next sc; sc in next sc; rep from * 5 times more—7 CLs. Ch 1, turn.

Row 3:
Sc in each st. Ch 1, turn.

Row 4:
Sc in first sc, CL in next sc; (sc in next sc, trc in next sc) 5 times; sc in next sc, CL in next sc; sc in next sc. Ch 1, turn.

Rows 5 through 12:
Rep Rows 3 and 4 four times more.

Row 13:
Rep Row 3.

Row 14:
Rep Row 2.

Row 15:
Sc in each st. Finish off.

Edging:
Hold motif with right side facing you and Row 15 at top; join blue in first sc.

Rnd 1:
Ch 1, in same sc work (sc, ch 2, sc)—corner made; sc in next 13 sc, in next sc work (sc, ch 2, sc)—corner made; working along next side in ends of rows, sk Row 15, sc in each of next 13 rows; working along lower edge in unused lps of beg ch, in first lp work (sc, ch 2, sc)—corner made; sc in next 13 lps, in next lp work (sc, ch 2, sc)—corner made; working along next side in ends of rows, sk Row 1, sc in each of next 13 rows; join in first sc.

Rnd 2:
Sl st in next ch-2 sp, ch 5 (counts as a dc and a ch-2 sp), dc in same sp—beg corner made; * † sk next sc, ch 1, (dc in next sc, ch 1, sk next sc) 7 times †; in next corner ch-2 sp work (dc, ch 2, dc)—corner made; rep from * twice more, then rep from † to † once; join in 3rd ch of beg ch-5.

Rnd 3:
Ch 1, sc in same ch as joining; * in next corner ch-2 sp work (sc, ch 2, sc); sc in each dc and in each ch-1 sp to next corner; rep from * twice more; in next corner ch-2 sp work (sc, ch 2, sc); sc in each dc and in each ch-1 sp to first sc; join in first sc.

Finish off and weave in all ends.

Strip Panel (make 4)
With variegated, ch 12.

Row 1 (wrong side):
Sc in 2nd ch from hook and in each rem ch—11 sc. Ch 1, turn.

Row 2 (right side):
Sc in first sc, CL in next sc; sc in next sc; * CL in next sc, sc in next sc; rep from * 3 times more—5 CLs. Ch 1, turn.

Row 3:
Sc in each st. Ch 1, turn.

Row 4:
Sc in first sc, CL in next sc; (sc in next sc, trc in next sc) 3 times; sc in next sc, CL in next sc; sc in next sc. Ch 1, turn.

Rows 5 through 172:
Rep Rows 3 and 4 eighty-four times more.

Row 173:
Rep Row 3.

Row 174:
Rep Row 2.

Row 175:
Sc in each st. Finish off.

Edging:
Hold strip panel with right side facing you and Row 175 at top; join blue in first sc.

Rnd 1:
Ch 1, in same sc work (sc, ch 2, sc)—corner made; sc in next 9 sc, in next sc work (sc, ch 2, sc)—corner made; working along next side in ends of rows, sk next row, sc in each of next 173 rows; working along lower edge in unused lps of beg ch, in first lp work (sc, ch 2, sc)—corner made; sc in next 9 lps, in next lp work (sc, ch 2, sc)—corner made; working along next side in ends of rows, sk next row, sc in each of next 173 rows; join in first sc.

Rnd 2:
Sl st in next ch-2 sp, ch 5 (counts as a dc and a ch-2 sp), dc in same sp—corner made; † sk next sc, ch 1, (dc in next sc, ch 1, sk next sc) 5 times; in next corner ch-2 sp work (dc, ch 2, dc)—corner made; sk next sc, ch 1, (dc in next sc, ch 1, sk next sc) 87 times †; in next corner ch-2 sp work (dc, ch 2, dc); rep from † to † once; join in 3rd ch of beg ch-5.

Rnd 3:
Ch 1, sc in same ch as joining; * in next corner ch-2 sp work (sc, ch 2, sc); sc in each dc and in each ch-1 sp to next corner; rep from * twice more; in next corner ch-2 sp work (sc, ch 2, sc); sc in each dc and in each ch-1 sp to first sc; join in first sc.

Finish off and weave in all ends.

Assembly
Join motifs in 3 panels of 9 motifs each. To join motifs, hold 2 motifs with right sides together and carefully matching stitches; with tapestry needle and blue, sew together with overcast stitch (see Stitch Guide on page 160) through BLs only along one side. Join remaining motifs together in same manner, having 9 motifs in each panel.

Join motif panels and strip panels together as follows:

Hold one strip panel and one motif panel with right sides together and carefully matching stitches; with tapestry needle and blue, sew together through BLs only along one long side. Referring to **Layout** for placement, sew remaining panels in same manner.

Layout

continued

Cheer Up

Border
Hold afghan with right side facing you and one short end at top. With blue make slip knot on hook and join with an sc in ch-2 sp in upper right-hand corner.

Rnd 1 (right side):
2 sc in same sp; working in BLs only, † sc in each sc and hdc in each joining to next corner ch-2 sp; 3 sc in corner ch-2 sp †; working along next side, sc in each sc to next corner ch-2 sp, 3 sc in corner ch-2 sp; working along next side, rep from † to † once; working along next side, sc in each sc to first sc; join in first sc.

Rnd 2:
Ch 1, sc in same sc and in each st to first sc; join in first sc.

Finish off and weave in ends.

Fringe
Following Fringe instructions on page 159, make Double Knot Fringe. Cut 30" strands of blue. Use 8 strands for each knot. Working across each short end of afghan, tie knots evenly spaced (about every 4th st). Trim ends even.

Diagonal Hues
designed by Diana Lynn Sippel

This afghan is easier than it looks! To get the dramatic diagonal rows, you simply start at one corner, increase stitches and change color each row until you reach the middle and then decrease each row until you reach the last corner.

Diagonal Hues

Size:
About 43" x 46"

Materials:
Worsted weight yarn, 14 oz (980 yds, 420 gms) black; 8 oz (560 yds, 240 gms) each, dk green, med green, lt green, rose, dk rose, and burgundy

Note: Our photographed afghan was made with Red Heart® Super Saver, Black #312, Hunter Green #389, Paddy Green #368, Grass Green #687, Claret #378, Rasberry #375, and Lt. Rasberry #744.

Size H (5mm) crochet hook, or size required for gauge
Size 16 tapestry needle

Gauge:
4 sc = 1"

Instructions

Note: To change color, work until 2 lps of last st remain on hook. With new color, YO and draw through 2 lps on hook. Cut old color.

With black, ch 4.

Row 1 (right side):
3 dc in 4th ch from hook, changing to dk green in last dc (beg 3 skipped chs count as a dc on this and following rows). Ch 4, turn.

Row 2:
3 dc in 4th ch from hook—beg block made, in sp formed by beg 3 skipped chs work (sc, ch 3, 3 dc) changing to med green in last dc—block made—2 blocks. Ch 4, turn.

Row 3:
3 dc in 4th ch from hook—beg block made; in next ch-3 sp work (sc, ch 3, 3 dc)—block made; in sp formed by beg 3 skipped chs work block, changing to lt green in last dc—3 blocks. Ch 4, turn.

Row 4:
Beg block in 4th ch from hook, block in each ch-3 sp and in sp formed by beg 3 skipped chs, changing to black in last dc—4 blocks. Ch 4, turn.

Rows 5 through 48:
Rep Row 4 in following color sequence, working 1 row of each color and having one additional block in each row until you have 48 blocks.

black
burgundy
rose
pink
black
dk green
med green
lt green

Row 49:
In each of next 47 ch-3 sps work block; sc in sp formed by beg 3 skipped chs, changing to dk green—47 blocks. Ch 3, turn.

Row 50:
In each of next 46 ch-3 sps work block; sc in sp formed by beg 3 skipped chs, changing to med green—46 blocks. Ch 3, turn.

Row 51:
In each of next 45 ch-3 sps work block; sc in sp formed by beg 3 skipped chs, changing to lt green—45 blocks. Ch 3, turn.

Row 52:
In each of next 44 ch-3 sps work block; sc in sp formed by beg 3 skipped chs, changing to black—44 blocks. Ch 3, turn.

Rows 53 through 95:
Work in pattern in following color sequence, working one row of each color and having one less block on each row until one block remains.

black

burgundy

rose

pink

black

dk green

med green

lt green

At end of last row, do not ch 3.

Finish off and weave in all ends.

Border
Hold afghan with right side facing you and first block made in upper right-hand corner; join black in unused lp of beg ch of first block.

Rnd 1:
Ch 1, 3 sc in same lp—corner made; working across side of blocks, 3 sc in side of each color block of first 48 rows; on Row 48, 3 sc in 3rd ch of turning ch—corner made; working across next side, 3 sc in side of each color block through Row 95; 3 sc in 3rd ch of turning ch-3—corner made; 3 sc in side of each color block through Row 48; 3 sc in 3rd dc of block—corner made; 3 sc in side of each color block through first block; join in first sc.

Rnd 2:
Ch 1, sc in same sc; 3 sc in next sc—corner made; * sc in each sc to 2nd sc of next corner, 3 sc in 2nd sc—corner made; rep from * twice more; sc in each sc to first sc; join in first sc. Finish off.

Rnd 3:
With burgundy make slip knot on hook and join with an sc in first sc of any corner; ch 1, sc in next sc, ch 1, sc in next sc, ch 1, sk next sc; * † sc in next sc, ch 1, sk next sc †; rep from † to † to first sc of next corner; sc in next sc, ch 1, sc in next sc, ch 1, sc in next sc, ch 1, sk next sc; rep from * twice more, then rep from † to † to joining sc; join in joining sc. Finish off.

Rnd 4:
With black make slip knot on hook and join with an sc in any ch-1 sp; ch 3; * sc in next ch-1 sp, ch 3; rep from * around; join in joining sc.

Finish off and weave in all ends.

I Love Scraps designed by Mary Ann Frits

If you're making an afghan to show someone you love them, this one is perfect! As you stitch this pattern using colorful scrap yarn, little rows of hearts appear.

Size:
About 42" x 62" before fringe

Materials:
Worsted weight yarn, 33½ oz (2345 yds, 1005 gms) off white; 32 oz (2240 yds, 960 gms) scraps

Note: Our photographed afghan was made with worsted weight yarn, 33½ oz (2345 yds, 1005 gms) off white and less than one skein each of 16 different colors.

Size H (5mm) crochet hook, or size required for gauge
Size 16 tapestry needle

Gauge:
11 dc = 3"

Pattern Stitch

Long Double Crochet (long dc):
Insert hook in st indicated and draw up to height of working row; YO and draw through 2 lps on hook— long dc made.

Instructions

Note: To change colors, work until 2 lps of last st remain on hook. With new color, YO and draw through 2 lps on hook. Cut old color.

With off white, ch 169.

Row 1 (right side):
Dc in 4th ch from hook (beg 3 skipped chs count as a dc) and in each rem ch, changing to any scrap color in last dc—167 dc. Cut off white. Ch 3 (counts as first dc on following rows), turn.

Row 2:
Dc in first dc, ch 2, sk next 5 dc; * in next dc work (2 dc, ch 1, 2 dc)—shell made; ch 2, sk next 6 dc; rep from * 21 times more; in next dc work (2 dc, ch 1, 2 dc)—shell made; ch 2, sk next 5 dc, 2 dc in 3rd ch of beg 3 skipped chs, changing to off white in last dc—23 shells. Ch 1, turn.

Row 3:
Sc in first dc, ch 1, sk next dc, working over next ch-2 sp, sk next unused dc on 2nd row below, long dc (see Pattern Stitch) in next 2 unused dc; * ch 2; on working row, sk next 2 dc, sc in next ch-1 sp, ch 2, sk next 2 dc, working over next ch-2 sp, sk next 2 unused dc on 2nd row below, long dc in next 2 unused dc; rep from * 22 times more; ch 1; on working row, sk next dc, sc in 3rd ch of turning ch-3. Ch 3, turn.

continued

I Love Scraps

Row 4:
Dc in in next ch-1 sp and in next 2 dc; * 2 dc in next ch-2 sp; dc in next sc, 2 dc in next ch-2 sp; dc in next 2 dc; rep from * 22 times more; dc in next ch-1 sp and in next sc, changing to new scrap color in last dc. Ch 3, turn.

Row 5:
Dc in first dc, ch 2, sk next 5 dc; * in next dc work shell; ch 2, sk next 6 dc; rep from * 21 times more; in next dc work shell; ch 2, sk next 5 dc, 2 dc in 3rd ch of turning ch-3, changing to off white in last dc. Ch 1, turn.

Rep Rows 3 through 5 until piece measures about 62", ending with a Row 4. At end of last row, do not ch 3.

Finish off and weave in all ends.

Fringe

Following Fringe instructions on page 159, make Single Knot Fringe. Cut 25" strands of off white; use 6 strands for each knot. Working across each short end of afghan, tie knots evenly spaced (about every 3rd st). Trim ends even.

Mountain Trails *designed by Rita Weiss*

*T*ramping through the mountains may be fun for hikers, but creating this ripple afghan is even more fun for crocheters. This versatile pattern is fun to give the outdoor-type person when crocheted with camouflage variegated as one of the yarns.

Mountain Trails

Size:
About 45" x 62"

Materials:
Worsted weight yarn, 27 oz (1890 yds, 810 gms) green;
22 oz (1540 yds, 660 gms) camouflage;
6 oz (420 yds, 180 gms) brown

Note: Our photographed model was made with Red Heart® Classic™, Camouflage #971, Lt Celery #615, Brown #7368.

Size H (5mm) crochet hook, or size required for gauge
Size 16 tapestry needle

Gauge:
7 dc = 1"

Pattern Stitch

Pebble Stitch (pebble st):
Draw up lp in st indicated, ch 3, keeping ch-3 to front of work, YO and draw through 2 lps on hook—pebble st made.

Instructions

Note: To change color, work until 2 lps of last st remain on hook. With new color, YO and draw through 2 lps on hook. Cut old color.

With camouflage, ch 237.

Row 1 (wrong side):
Sc in 2nd ch from hook and in next 4 chs, 3 sc in next ch; * sc in next 3 chs, sk next 2 chs, sc in next 3 chs, 3 sc in next ch; rep from * to last 5 chs; sc in last 5 chs. Ch 1, turn.

Row 2 (right side):
Working in BLs only, dec over first 2 sc (to work dec: draw up lp in each of next 2 sts, YO and draw through all 3 lps on hook—dec made); sc in next 4 sc, 3 sc in next sc; * sc in next 3 sc, sk next 2 sc, sc in next 3 sc, 3 sc in next sc; rep from * to last 6 sc; sc in next 4 sc, dec over last 2 sc. Ch 1, turn.

Rows 3 through 5:
Rep Row 2. At end of Row 5, change to brown; cut camouflage. Ch 1, turn.

Row 6:
Working through both lps, sl st loosely in each sc, changing to green in last sc. Ch 1, turn.

Row 7:
Leaving sl sts of prev row unworked and working in BLs only of Row 5, rep Row 2.

Row 8:
Working through both lps, dec; sc in next 4 sc, in next sc work [pebble st (see Pattern Stitch), sc, pebble st]; * sc in next 3 sc, sk next 2 sc, sc in next 3 sc, in next sc work (pebble st, sc, pebble st); rep from * to last 6 sc; sc in next 4 sc, dec. Ch 1, turn.

Row 9:
Dec; sc in next 4 sts, 3 sc in next st; * sc in next 3 sts, sk next 2 sts, sc in next 3 sts, 3 sc in next st; rep from * to last 6 sts; sc in next 4 sts, dec. Ch 1, turn.

Row 10:
Dec; sc in next 2 sc, pebble st in next sc; sc in next sc, in next sc work (pebble st, sc, pebble st); * sc in next sc, pebble st in next sc; sc in next sc, sk next 2 sc, sc in next sc, pebble st in next sc; sc in next sc, in next sc work (pebble st, sc, pebble st); rep from * to last 6 sc; sc in next sc, pebble st in next sc; sc in next 2 sc, dec. Ch 1, turn.

Row 11:
Rep Row 9, changing to brown. Ch 1, turn.

Row 12:
Sl st loosely in each sc. Change to camouflage, by drawing lp through; cut brown. Ch 1, turn.

Row 13:
Leaving sl sts of prev row unworked and working in BLs only of Row 11, dec; sc in next 4 sc, 3 sc in next sc; * sc in next 3 sc, sk next 2 sc, sc in next 3 sc, 3 sc in next sc; rep from * to last 6 sc; sc in next 4 sc, dec. Ch 1, turn.

Row 14:
Working in BLs only, dec; sc in next 4 sc, 3 sc in next sc; * sc in next 3 sc, sk next 2 sc, sc in next 3 sc, 3 sc in next sc; rep from * to last 6 sc; sc in next 4 sc, dec. Ch 1, turn.

Rows 15 through 134:
Rep Rows 3 through 14 fourteen times more.

Rows 135 through 137:
Rep Rows 3 through 5.

Finish off and weave in all ends.

Shady Glen
designed by Eleanor Albano-Miles

For a quick-to-make, very portable afghan you can't go wrong with this easy afghan. Crocheted in strips using a variegated yarn and two contrasting colors even beginners will enjoy it.

Size:
About 54" x 68"

Materials:
Worsted weight yarn, 22 oz (1540 yds, 660 gms) variegated; 12 oz (840 yds, 360 gms) brown; 17 oz (1190 yds, 510 gms) tan

Note: *Our photographed afghan was made with Caron® Simply Soft®, Green Meadow Ombre #2711, Cedar #2667, and Bone #2604.*

Size J (6mm) crochet hook, or size required for gauge
Size 16 tapestry needle

Gauge:
7 sc = 2"

Instructions

Panel (make 6)
With variegated, ch 186.

Row 1 (right side):
Dc in 6th ch from hook (5 skipped chs count as a ch 1, a dc, and a ch-1 sp); * ch 1, sk next ch, dc in next ch; rep from * 89 times more—91 ch-1 sps and 92 dc. Ch 4 (counts as first dc and ch-1 sp on following rows), turn.

Row 2:
* Dc in next dc, ch 1; rep from * 90 times more; dc in 4th ch of beg 5 skipped chs. Ch 4, turn.

Row 3:
* Dc in next dc, ch 1; rep from * 90 times more; dc in 3rd ch of turning ch-4. Ch 1, do not turn.

Note: *Remainder of panel is worked in rnds.*

Rnd 1:
Working along short end, 2 sc in sp made by last dc; † sc in side of next edge st, sc in sp made by same st, sc in side of next edge st, in sp made by next edge st work (2 sc, ch 2, 2 sc)—corner made †; working along next side in unused lps of beg ch and in sps made by skipped chs, sc in next lp, (sc in next ch-1 sp and in next lp) 89 times; in sp made by turning ch work (2 sc, ch 2, 2 sc)—corner made; working along next short edge, rep from † to † once; working across Row 3, sc in next dc, (sc in next ch-1 sp and in next dc) 89 times; 2 sc in same sp as beg 2 sc; ch 2—corner made; join in first sc—183 sc on each long side and 7 sc on each short side. Finish off.

continued

Shady Glen

Rnd 2:
Hold panel with wrong side facing you and one long edge at top; join brown in upper right-hand corner ch-2 sp; ch 1, in same sp work (sc, trc, sc)—corner made; working in FLs only, † sc in next sc, trc in next sc, (sc in next 2 sc, trc in next sc) 60 times; sc in next sc, in next corner ch-2 sp work (sc, trc, sc)—corner made; (sc in next sc, trc in next sc) 3 times; sc in next sc †; in next corner ch-2 sp work (sc, trc, sc)—corner made; rep from † to † once; join in first sc. Finish off.

Rnd 3:
Hold panel with right side facing you and one long side at top; join tan in trc in upper right-hand corner; ch 1, in same trc work (hdc, ch 2, hdc)—corner made; hdc in each st to next corner trc; * in corner trc work (hdc, ch 2, hdc)—corner made; hdc in each st to next corner trc; rep from * twice more; join in first hdc. Finish off.

Rnd 4:
Hold panel with right side facing you and one long side at top; join variegated in ch-2 sp in upper right-hand corner, ch 1, in same sp work (sc, ch 2, sc)—corner made; working in BLs only, sc in each hdc to next corner ch-2 sp; * in corner ch-2 sp work (sc, ch 2, sc)—corner made; sc in each hdc to next corner ch-2 sp; rep from * twice more; join in first sc. Ch 4 (counts as a dc and ch-1 sp on following rnd), turn.

Rnd 5:
Sk next sc, dc in next sc; † ch 1, sk next sc, dc in next sc †; rep from † to † to next corner ch-2 sp; ch 1, in corner ch-2 sp work (dc, ch 2, dc)—corner made; ch 1, dc in next sc; rep from † to † to next corner ch-2 sp; ch 1, in corner ch-2 sp work (dc, ch 2, dc)—corner made; ch 1, dc in next sc; rep from † to † to next corner ch-2 sp; ch 1, in corner ch-2 sp work (dc, ch 2, dc);. ch 1, dc in next sc; rep from † to † to next corner ch-2 sp; ch 1, in corner ch-2 sp work (dc, ch 2, dc); ch 1; join in 3rd ch of turning ch-4. Ch 1, turn.

Rnd 6:
Sc in same ch as joining, in next ch-1 sp, and in next dc; * † in next corner ch-2 sp work (sc, ch 2, sc)—corner made †; sc in each dc and in each ch-1 sp to next corner ch-2 sp; rep from * twice more, then rep from † to † once; sc in each dc and in each ch-1 sp to first sc; join in first sc. Finish off.

Rnd 7:
Hold panel with wrong side facing you and one long side at top; join brown in ch-2 sp in upper right-hand corner, ch 1, in same sp work (sc, trc, sc)—corner made; † sc in next sc, (trc in next sc, sc in next 2 sc) 64 times; trc in next sc, sc in next sc, in next corner ch-2 sp work (sc, trc, sc)—corner made; (trc in next sc, sc in next 2 sc) 6 times; trc in next sc †; in next corner ch-2 sp work (sc, trc, sc)—corner made; rep from † to † once more; join in first sc. Finish off.

Rnd 8:
Hold panel with right side facing you and one long side at top; join tan in trc in upper right-hand corner; ch 1, in same trc work (hdc, ch 2, hdc)—corner made; hdc in each st to next corner trc; * † in corner trc work (hdc, ch 2, hdc)—corner made †; hdc in each st to next corner trc; rep from * once more, then rep from † to † once; hdc in each st to first hdc; join in BL of first hdc.

Rnd 9:
Ch 1, working in BLs only, sc in same hdc; * † in next corner ch-2 sp work (sc, ch 2, sc)—corner made †; sc in each hdc to next corner; rep from * twice more, then rep from † to † once; sc in each hdc to first sc; join in first sc.
Finish off and weave in all ends.

Assembly

Hold 2 panels with right sides together and stitches in same direction. With tapestry needle and tan, sew panels together with overcast stitch (see Stitch Guide on page 160) through BLs only. Join remaining panels in same manner.

Border

Hold afghan with right side facing you and one short end at top; join tan in upper right-hand corner ch-2 sp; in same sp work (sc, ch 2, sc)—corner made; † sc in each sc to next ch-2 sp, hdc in ch-2 sp, dc in joining, hdc in next ch-2 sp †; rep from † to † 4 times more; sc in each sc to next corner ch-2 sp, in ch-2 sp work (sc, ch 2, sc)—corner made; sc in each sc along next side to next corner ch-2 sp, in ch-2 sp work (sc, ch 2, sc)—corner made; rep from † to † 5 times; sc in each sc to next corner ch-2 sp, in ch-2 sp work (sc, ch 2, sc)—corner made; sc in each sc along next side to first sc; join in first sc.

Finish off and weave in ends.

Spring Waves
designed by Eleanor Albano-Miles

Just as the sun hits the ocean waves on a bright spring day, this afghan is a joy to behold. First three shades of yarn are crocheted in stripes, and then the waves are added for interesting dimension.

Spring Waves

Size:
About 42" x 65"

Materials:
Worsted weight yarn, 31 oz (2170 yds, 930 gms) lt green;
22 oz (1540 yds, 660 gms) med green;
27 oz (1890 yds, 810 gms) dk green

Note: Our photographed afghan was made with Wintuk® Mist Green #3187, Medium Fir #3260, and Fir #3010.

Size I (5.5mm) crochet hook, or size required for gauge
Size 16 tapestry needle

Gauge:
7 sc = 2"

Pattern Stitch

Front Post Single Crochet (FPsc):
Insert hook from front to back to front around post of (see Stitch Guide on page 160) st indicated; YO and draw up lp, YO and draw through both lps on hook—FPsc made.

Instructions

Note: To change color, work until 2 lps of last st remain on hook. With new color, YO and draw through 2 lps on hook. Cut old color.

With lt green, ch 154.

Row 1 (right side):
Sc in 2nd ch from hook and in each rem ch—153 sc. Ch 3 (counts as first dc on following rows), turn.

Row 2:
Dc in each sc, changing to med green in last dc. Ch 1, turn.

Row 3:
Sc in each dc and in 3rd ch of turning ch-3. Ch 1, turn.

Row 4:
Sc in each sc. Ch 1, turn.

Rows 5 through 7:
Rep Row 4. At end of Row 7, do not ch 1. Ch 3, turn.

Row 8:
Dc in each sc, changing to dk green in last dc. Ch 1, turn.

Rows 9 through 14:
Rep Rows 3 through 8, changing to lt green at end of Row 14.

Rows 15 through 20:
Rep Rows 3 through 8, changing to med green at end of Row 20.

Rows 21 through 200:
Rep Rows 3 through 20 ten times more.

Rows 201 through 212:
Rep Rows 3 through 14. At end of Row 212, do not change color.

Row 213:
Sc in each dc and in 3rd ch of turning ch-3.

Finish off and weave in all ends.

Wave Trim

Hold afghan with right side facing you and beg ch at top; join lt green around post **(see Stitch Guide on page 160)** of 2nd dc on Row 2 from right.

Row 1 (right side):
Ch 1, FPsc **(see Pattern Stitch)** around same dc as joining; FPsc around post of each rem dc to last dc. Ch 6 **(counts as first dc and picot on following row)**, turn, leaving rem dc unworked.

Row 2:
Sl st in 3rd ch from hook—picot made; 3 dc in first sc; * sk next 5 sc, in next sc work **(3 dc, ch 3, sl st in 3rd ch from hook, 3 dc)**—shell made; rep from * 23 times more; sk next 5 sc, in next sc work **(3 dc, ch 3, sl st in 3rd ch from hook, dc)**. Finish off.

With matching yarn, repeat shell trim on all dc rows.

Weave in all ends.

Themes and Variations
designed by Eleanor Albano-Miles

This distinctive afghan is a handsome addition to any room. The variegated zigzag rows are added to a plain background to give the surface special allure.

Size:
About 44" x 62"

Materials:
Worsted weight yarn, 42 oz (2940 yds, 1260 gms) off white; 13 oz (910 yds, 390 gms) variegated

Note: *Our photographed afghan was made with Red Heart® Soft, New Aran #7313 and Floral #7935.*
Size I (5.5mm) crochet hook, or size required for gauge
Size 16 tapestry needle

Gauge:
7 dc = 2"

Instructions

Base
With off white, ch 148.

Row 1 (wrong side):
Sc in 2nd ch from hook and in each rem ch—147 sc. Ch 3 (counts as first dc on following rows), turn.

Row 2 (right side):
Dc in each sc. Ch 1, turn.

Row 3:
Sc in each dc and in 3rd ch of turning ch-3. Ch 3, turn.

Rows 4 through 171:
Rep Rows 2 and 3 eighty-four times. At end of Row 171, do not ch 3.

Finish off and weave in all ends.

Trim Rows
Hold base with right side facing you and Row 171 at top; with variegated make slip knot on hook and join with an sc around post (see Stitch Guide on page 160) of 2nd dc on Row 6.

Row 1:
*† Ch 1, working upward, sk sc row, sc around post of next dc on next row above †; rep from † to † once more; ch 1, working downward, sk sc row, sc around post of 2nd dc from worked dc on next row below; ch 1, working downward, sk sc row, sc around post of 4th dc from worked dc on next row below; rep from * 35 times more. Finish off.

Row 2:
Join variegated around post of 2nd dc on Row 10, ch 1, sc around same dc; *† ch 1, working upward and to the left, sk sc row, sc around post of next dc on next row above †; rep from † to † once more; ch 1, working downward and to the left, sk sc row, sc around post of 2nd dc from worked dc on next row below; ch 1, working downward, sk sc row, sc around post of 4th dc from worked dc on next row below; rep from * 35 times more. Finish off.

Rep Row 2, joining around post of 2nd dc on highest row worked, and moving upward with each repeat. Leave last 5 rows unworked.

Weave in all ends.

Border
Hold afghan with wrong side facing you and one long edge at top; with off white make slip knot on hook and join with an sc in edge of sc row in upper right-hand corner.

Row 1 (wrong side):
Working in ends of dc rows only, in sps formed by edge dc and turning chs, 2 sc in each sp across; sc in edge of last sc row—172 sc. Ch 2 (counts as a dc), turn.

Row 2 (right side):
Dc in each sc. Ch 1, turn.

Row 3:
Sc in each dc and in 2nd ch of turning ch-2. Ch 2, turn.

Row 4:
Dc in each sc. Ch 1, turn.

Row 5:
Sc in each dc.

Finish off and weave in ends.

Repeat on other long side.

Color Me Happy
designed by Mary Lamb Becker

*K*ids of all ages will love the upbeat charm of this cozy wrap. Crocheted from side to side, the colorful bobbles are a variegated yarn.

Size:
About 46" x 62" before fringe

Materials:
Worsted weight yarn, 57 oz (3990 yds, 1710 gms) off white; 4 oz (280 yds, 120 gms) variegated

Note: *Our photographed afghan was made with Red Heart® Super Saver, Soft White #316 and Mexicana # 950.*

Size I (5.5mm) crochet hook, or size required for gauge
Size 16 tapestry needle

Gauge:
3 dc = 1"

Instructions
Note: *Afghan is worked side-to-side.*

With off white, ch 182.

Row 1 (wrong side):
Sc in 2nd ch from hook and in each rem ch—181 sc. Ch 3 (counts as first dc on following rows), turn.

Row 2 (right side):
Dc in each sc. Ch 1, turn.

Row 3:
Sc in each dc and in 3rd ch of turning ch-3. Ch 3, turn.

Row 4:
Dc in each sc. Ch 1, turn.

Row 5:
Sc in each dc and in 3rd ch of turning ch-3. Ch 1, turn.

Row 6:
Working in FLs only, sc in first sc; * ch 1, sk next sc, sc in next sc; rep from * across. Ch 1, turn.

Row 7:
Working in unused lps of worked sc on Row 5 and in FLs only of skipped sc of same row, sc in each sc. Ch 3, turn.

Row 8:
Dc in each sc. Ch 1, turn.

Row 9:
Sc in each dc and in 3rd ch of turning ch-3. Drop off white; do not cut.

Hold piece with wrong side facing you; with variegated make a slip knot on hook and join with an sc in BL only of 2nd sc on prev row.

Row 10:
Working in BLs only, 2 sc in same lp as joining; * ch 2, sk next sc, 3 sc in next sc; rep from * to last sc. Finish off, leaving rem sc unworked. With off white, ch 1, turn.

continued

Color Me Happy

Row 11:
Sc through both lps of first sc; working behind prev row, * sc in unused lp of next sc, working over next ch-2 sp, sc through both lps of next skipped sc; rep from * 88 times more; working behind prev row, sc through unused lp of next sc, sc in both lps of next sc. Ch 1, turn.

Row 12:
Sc in each sc. Ch 3, turn.

Row 13:
Dc in each sc. Ch 1, turn.

Row 14:
Sc in each dc and in 3rd ch of turning ch-3. Ch 1, turn.

Row 15:
Working in FLs only, sc in first sc; * ch 1, sk next sc, sc in next sc; rep from * across. Ch 1, turn.

Rows 16 through 33:
Rep Rows 7 through 15 twice more.

Row 34:
Rep Row 7.

Row 35:
Rep Row 4.

Rows 36 through 93:
Rep Rows 3 and 4 twenty-nine times.

Row 94:
Rep Row 3.

Row 95:
Rep Row 6.

Rows 96 through 122:
Rep Rows 7 through 15 three times.

Row 123:
Rep Row 7.

Row 124:
Rep Row 4.

Row 125 and 126:
Rep Rows 3 and 4.

Row 127:
Rep Row 3. At end of row, do not ch 3.

Finish off and weave in all ends.

Edging

Hold afghan with right side facing you and one short end at top and Row 1 to right; join off white in edge of Row 1, ch 3 (counts as a dc); working in ends of rows in sps formed by edge sts and turning chs, work 2 dc in each dc row and work dc in each sc row and in each raised sc row.

Repeat on opposite short end.

Fringe

Following Fringe instructions on page 159, make Single Knot Fringe. Cut 25" strands of each color; use 5 strands for each knot. Working across each short end of afghan, tie knots of matching colors evenly spaced (about every 3rd st). Trim ends even.

Garden Florals

*R*oses and lilies, peonies and blossoms—if you're a romantic, these luscious afghans are for you. This section includes light and lacy afghans and warm cozy wraps. Delight your loved ones using the language of flowers!

Blanket of Peonies 34
Castle Grounds 38
Day Lilies 43
Parlor Bouquet 47
Rose Dreams 50
Wedding Roses 53
Wearing of the Green . . . 56

Blanket of Peonies
designed by Diana Lynn Sippel

The three-dimensional flowers are blooming with delight. Combined with plain squares, this afghan will add beauty to your surroundings.

Size:
About 38" x 53"

Materials:
Worsted weight yarn, 20 oz (1400 yds, 600 gms) white; 10 oz (700 yds, 300 gms) green; 6 oz (420 yds, 180 gms) each, med rose and lt rose; 2 oz (140 yds, 60 gms) dk rose

Note: Our photographed afghan was made with Red Heart® Super Saver, White #311, Dark Spruce #361, Rasberry #375, Lt Rasberry #774, and Claret #378.

Size H (5mm) crochet hook, or size required for gauge
Size 16 tapestry needle

Gauge:
7 sc = 2"

Pattern Stitches

Long Double Crochet (long dc):
YO, insert hook in sp indicated, draw up lp to height of working rnd, (YO, draw through 2 lps on hook) twice—long dc made.

Long Half Double Crochet (long hdc):
YO, insert hook in sp indicated, draw up lp to height of working rnd, (YO, draw through all 3 lps on hook)—long hdc made.

Instructions

Flower Square (make 18)
With dk rose, ch 5; join to form a ring.

Rnd 1 (right side):
Ch 1, 16 sc in ring; join in first sc.

Rnd 2:
Ch 1, sc in same sc and in next sc; ch 2; * sc in next 2 sc, ch 2; rep from * 6 times more; join in first sc.

Rnd 3:
Ch 1, sc in same sc and in next sc, ch 3; * sc in next 2 sc, ch 3; rep from * 6 times more; join in first sc.

Rnd 4:
Ch 1, dec over first 2 sc (to work dec: draw up lp in each of next 2 sts, YO and draw through all 3 lps on hook—dec made); ch 3; * dec over next 2 sc; ch 3; rep from * 6 times more; join in first dec—8 sc. Finish off.

continued

Blanket of Peonies

Rnd 5:
Join white in any sc; ch 1, 3 sc in same sc—corner made; 4 sc in next ch-3 sp; sk next sc, 4 sc in next ch-3 sp; * 3 sc in next sc—corner made; 4 sc in next ch-3 sp; sk next sc, 4 sc in next ch-3 sp; rep from * around; join in first sc.

Rnd 6:
Ch 1, sc in same sc; * corner in next sc; sc in next 10 sc; rep from * twice more; corner in next sc; sc in next 9 sc; join in first sc.

Rnd 7:
Ch 1, sc in same sc and in next sc; * corner in next sc; sc in next 12 sc; rep from * twice more; corner in next sc; sc in next 10 sc; join in first sc.

Rnd 8:
Ch 1, sc in same sc and in next 2 sc; * corner in next sc; sc in next 14 sc; rep from * twice more; corner in next sc; sc in next 11 sc; join in first sc. Finish off.

Rnd 9:
With green make slip knot on hook and join with an sc in first sc to left of joining, ch 1; working over next 5 sc, in 2nd sc of corner on 3rd rnd below work [2 long hdc (see Pattern Stitches on page 35), long dc (see Pattern Stitches on page 35), 2 long hdc]; * ch 1, sk next sc, (sc in next sc, ch 1, sk next sc) 6 times; working over next 5 sc, in 2nd sc of next corner on 3rd rnd below work (2 long hdc, long dc, 2 long hdc); rep from * twice more; ch 1, sk next sc, (sc in next sc, ch 1, sk next sc) 5 times; join in first sc. Finish off.

Rnd 10:
Join white in any long dc; ch 1, corner in same st; sc in next 2 long hdc; * † 2 sc in each of next 7 ch-1 sps; sc in next 2 long hdc †; corner in next long dc, sc in next 2 long hdc; rep from * twice more, then rep from † to † once; join in first sc. Finish off.

Rnd 11:
With green make slip knot on hook, join with an sc in BL of 2nd sc of any corner; 2 sc in same lp; * working in BLs only, sc in each sc to 2nd sc of next corner; corner in next sc; rep from * twice more; sc in each sc to first sc; join in first sc. Finish off.

Inner Flower Ring:
Join lt rose in any ch-2 sp of Rnd 2; ch 2 (counts as an hdc), in same sp work (3 dc, hdc); * in next ch-2 sp work (hdc, 3 dc, hdc); rep from * to beg ch-2; join in 2nd ch of beg ch. Finish off.

Outer Flower Ring:
Join med rose in any ch-3 sp of Rnd 3; ch 3 (counts as a dc), in same sp work (5 trc, dc); * in next ch-3 sp work (dc, 5 trc, dc); rep from * to beg ch-3; join in 3rd ch of beg ch. Finish off and weave in all ends.

Filet Square (make 17)
With white, ch 16.

Row 1 (right side):
Sc in 2nd ch from hook and in each rem ch—15 sc. Ch 2, turn.

Row 2:
Sk first sc, sc in next sc, (ch 1, sk next sc, sc in next sc) 6 times; ch 1, sc in next sc. Ch 1, turn.

Row 3:
2 sc in each of next 7 ch-1 sps; 2 sc in sp formed by turning ch-2—16 sc. Ch 2, turn.

Row 4:
Sk first sc, sc in next sc, (ch 1, sk next sc, sc in next sc) 7 times. Ch 1, turn.

Rows 5 through 14:
Rep Rows 3 and 4 five times more.

Row 15:
Rep Row 3. At end of row, do not ch 2. Ch 1.

Edging:
Rnd 1:
Working along next side in ends of rows, 3 sc in Row 15—corner made; sc in next 13 rows, 3 sc in next row—corner made; working in unused lps of beg ch, sk first lp, sc in next 13 lps, sk next lp; working along next side in ends of rows, 3 sc in Row 1—corner made; sc in next 13 rows, 3 sc in next row—corner made; sc in next 13 sc; join in first sc.

Rnd 2:
Ch 1, sc in same sc; corner in next sc; * sc in next 15 sc, corner in next sc; rep from * twice more; sc in next 14 sc; join in first sc. Finish off.

Rnd 3:
Join green in 2nd sc of any corner; ch 1, corner in same sc; * † (ch 1, sk next sc, sc in next sc) 8 times; ch 1, sk next sc †; corner in next sc; rep from * twice more, then rep from † to † once; join in first sc. Finish off.

Rnd 4:
Join white in 2nd sc of any corner; ch 1, corner in same sc; * 2 sc in each ch-1 sp to next corner; corner in 2nd sc of next corner; rep from * twice more; 2 sc in each ch-1 sp to first sc; join in first sc. Finish off.

Rnd 5:

Join green in 2nd sc of any corner; ch 1, corner in same sc; * sc in next 20 sc, corner in next sc; rep from * twice more; sc in next 20 sc; join in first sc.

Finish off and weave in all ends.

Assembly

Referring to **Layout** for placement of squares, join squares in 5 rows of 7 squares each. To join squares, hold 2 squares with right sides together and carefully matching stitches; with tapestry needle and green, sew together with overcast stitch **(see Stitch Guide on page 160)** through BLs only along one side. Join squares in rows, then join rows together in same manner, making sure all four-corner junctions are firmly joined.

Border

Hold afghan with right side facing you and one short end at top; join green in 2nd sc in upper right-hand corner.

Rnd 1:

Ch 1, 3 sc in same sc—corner made; † sc in next 22 sc and in next joining †; rep from † to † 3 times more; sc in next 22 sc, 3 sc in next sc—corner made; rep from † to † 6 times; sc in next 22 sc, 3 sc in next sc—corner made; rep from † to † 4 times; sc in next 22 sc, corner in next sc; rep from † to † 6 times; sc in next 22 sc; join in first sc. Finish off.

Rnd 2:

Join white in 2nd sc of any corner; ch 1, sc in same sc, ch 3, sk next sc; * sc in next sc, ch 3, sk next sc; rep from * around; join in first sc.

Finish off and weave in all ends.

Layout

Castle Grounds *designed by Linda Mershon*

Size:
About 46" x 58"

Materials:
Worsted weight yarn, 23 oz (1610 yds, 690 gms) off white; 14 oz (980 yds, 420 gms) green, 2 oz (140 yds, 60 gms) blue; 1 oz (70 yds, 30 gms) each, pink and yellow

Note: Our photographed afghan was made with Caron Wintuk, Off White #3002, Medium Fir #3260, Sky #3254, Tea Rose #3257, and Jonquil #3256.

Size H (5mm) crochet hook, or size required for gauge
Size 16 tapestry needle

Gauge:
7 sc = 2"

Pattern Stitch

Cluster (CL):
Keeping last lp of each dc on hook, dc in each of next 2 sts indicated, YO and draw through all 3 lps on hook—CL made.

Instructions

First Motif

Flower:
With blue, ch 2.

Rnd 1 (right side):
8 sc in 2nd ch from hook; join in FL of first sc.

Rnd 2:
Ch 1, in same lp work (sc, hdc, dc, hdc, sc)—petal made; working in FLs only, in each rem sc work (sc, hdc, dc, hdc, sc)—petal made; join in first sc—8 petals.

Rnd 3:
Ch 2, working in unused lps of Rnd 1, * sl st in next lp, ch 2; rep from * around; join in BL of same sc as joining. Finish off.

Square:
Rnd 1:
Join off white in any ch-2 sp on flower, ch 1, sc in same sp, ch 3, dc in next ch-2 sp, ch 3, (sc in next ch-2 sp, ch 3, dc in next ch-2 sp, ch 3) 3 times; join in first sc.

continued

The organized beauty of a formal garden inspired this gorgeous afghan. Three dimensional flowers at the center of each join-as-you-go square are made in a variety of colors making it as pretty as a spring bouquet.

Castle Grounds

Rnd 2:
Ch 1, sc in same sc; ch 1, sk next ch, sc in next ch, ch 1, sk next ch; * † in next dc work (sc, ch 2, sc)—corner made; ch 1, sk next ch, sc in next ch, ch 1, sk next ch †; sc in next sc, ch 1, sk next ch, sc in next ch, ch 1, sk next ch; rep from * twice more, then rep from † to † once; join in first sc.

Rnd 3:
Sl st in next ch-1 sp, ch 1, sc in same sp; ch 1, sc in next ch-1 sp, ch 1, in next ch-2 sp work (sc, ch 2, sc)—corner made; * ch 1, (sc in next ch-1 sp, ch 1) 4 times; in next ch-2 sp work (sc, ch 2, sc)—corner made; rep from * twice more; ch 1, (sc in next ch-1 sp, ch 1) twice; join in first sc.

Rnd 4:
Sl st in next ch-1 sp, ch 1, sc in same sp; ch 1, sc in next ch-1 sp, ch 1; * † corner in ch-2 sp of next corner; ch 1 †; (sc in next ch-1 sp, ch 1) 5 times; rep from * twice more, then rep from † to † once; (sc in next ch-1 sp, ch 1) 3 times; join in first sc.

Rnd 5:
Sl st in next ch-1 sp, ch 1, sc in same sp; ch 1, sc in next ch-1 sp, ch 1; * † corner in next corner; ch 1 †; (sc in next ch-1 sp, ch 1) 6 times; rep from * twice more, then rep from † to † once; (sc in next ch-1 sp, ch 1) 4 times; join in first sc.

Rnd 6:
Sl st in next ch-1 sp, ch 1, (sc in next ch-1 sp, ch 1) twice; corner in next corner; ch 1; * (sc in next ch-1 sp, ch 1) 7 times; corner in next corner; rep from * twice more; (sc in next ch-1 sp, ch 1) 5 times; join in first sc. Finish off.

Rnd 7:
Join green in any corner ch-2 sp, ch 1, 3 sc in same sp—corner made; * working in each sc and in each ch-1 sp, sc in next 17 sts, 3 sc in next corner ch-2 sp—corner made; rep from * twice more; sc in next 17 sts; join in first sc.

Rnd 8:
Ch 1, sc in same sc; * 3 sc in next sc—corner made; sc in next 19 sc; rep from * twice more; 3 sc in next sc—corner made; sc in next 18 sc; join in first sc. Finish off.

Rnd 9:
Join off white in 2nd sc of any corner; ch 1, in same sc work (sc, ch 1, sc)—corner made; ch 1, sk next sc; * † (sc in next sc, ch 1, sk next sc) 10 times †; in next sc work (sc, ch 1, sc)—corner made; rep from * twice more, then rep from † to † once; join in first sc.

Rnd 10:
Sl st in next ch-1 sp, ch 1, in same sp work (sc, ch 2, sc)—corner made; * (ch 1, sc in next ch-1 sp) 11 times; ch 1, in next corner ch-1 sp work (sc, ch 2, sc)—corner made; rep from * twice more; (ch 1, sc in next ch-1 sp) 11 times; ch 1; join in first sc.

Rnd 11:
Sl st in next ch-2 sp, ch 1, in same sp work (sc, ch 2, sc)—corner made; * ch 1, (sc in next ch-1 sp, ch 1) 12 times; in next ch-2 sp work (sc, ch 2, sc)—corner made; rep from * twice more; ch 1, (sc in next ch-1 sp, ch 1) 12 times; join in first sc. Finish off.

Rnd 12:
Join green in any corner ch-2 sp, ch 1, in same sp work (sc, ch 7, sc)—corner made; * (ch 3, sc in next ch-1 sp) 13 times; ch 3; in next corner ch-2 sp work (sc, ch 7, sc)—corner made; rep from * twice more; ch 3, (sc in next ch-1 sp, ch 3) 13 times; join in first sc. Finish off.

Flower Trim:
Join blue around post (see Stitch Guide on page 160) of any sc on Rnd 1 behind petals; ch 1, sc around same post, ch 3; (sc around post of next st, ch 3) 7 times; join in first sc.

Finish off and weave in all ends.

Second Motif

Flower:
With pink, ch 2.

Rnds 1 through 3:
Rep Rnds 1 through 3 of First Motif

Square:
Rnds 1 through 11:
Rep Rnds 1 through 11 of First Motif.

Rnd 12 (joining rnd):
Join green in any corner ch-2 sp, ch 1, in same sp work (sc, ch 7, sc)—corner made; ch 3, (sc in next ch-1 sp, ch 3) 13 times; * in next corner ch-2 sp work (sc, ch 7, sc)—corner made; ch 3, (sc in next ch-1 sp, ch 3) 13 times; rep from * once more; sc in next corner ch-2 sp, ch 3; hold wrong side of completed motif facing wrong side of working motif; sl st in any corner ch-7 lp on completed motif; ch 3; on working motif, sc in same sp—joined corner made; ch 3, (sc in next ch-1 sp, ch 3) 13 times; join in first sc. Finish off.

Flower Trim:
Join pink around post of any sc on Rnd 1 behind petals; ch 1, sc around same post, ch 3; (sc around post of next st, ch 3) 7 times; join in first sc.

Finish off and weave in all ends.

Third Motif

Work same as Second Motif through Rnd 11 of Square.

Rnd 12 (joining rnd):
Join green in any corner ch-2 sp, ch 1, in same sp work (sc, ch 7, sc)—corner made; ch 3, (sc in next ch-1 sp, ch 3) 13 times; * in next corner ch-2 sp work (sc, ch 7, sc)—corner made; ch 3, (sc in next ch-1 sp, ch 3) 13 times; rep from * once more; sc in next corner ch-2 sp, ch 3; hold

wrong side of completed motif facing wrong side of working motif; sl st in ch-7 sp on corner opposite joined corner of completed motif; ch 3; on working motif, sc in same sp, ch 3, (sc in next ch-1 sp, ch 3) 13 times; join in first sc. Finish off.

Flower Trim:
Join pink around post of any sc on Rnd 1 behind petals; ch 1, sc around same post, ch 3; (sc around post of next st, ch 3) 7 times; join in first sc.

Finish off and weave in all ends.

Fourth Motif
With blue, work same as Third Motif.

> **Note:** Referring to Layout, you have now completed Row 1.

Fifth Motif
With yellow, work same as First Motif through Rnd 11 of Square.

Rnd 12 (joining rnd): Join green in any corner ch-2 sp, ch 1, in same sp work (sc, ch 7, sc)—corner made; ch 3; (sc in next ch-1 sp, ch 3) 13 times; sc in next ch-2 sp, ch 3; hold wrong side of first motif facing wrong side of working motif; on completed motif, sl st in corner ch-7 sp, ch 3; on working motif, sc in same sp; † ch 1; on completed motif, sl st in next ch-3 sp, ch 1; on working motif, sc in next ch-1 sp †; rep from † to † 13 times more; ch 3; on completed motif, sl st in next corner joining, ch 3; on working motif, sc in same sp; rep from † to † 14 times; ch 3; on completed motif, sl st in next corner ch-7 sp, ch 3; on working motif, sc in same sp; ch 3; (sc in next ch-1 sp, ch 3) 13 times; join in first sc. Finish off.

Flower Trim:
Join yellow around post of any sc on Rnd 1 behind petals; ch 1, sc around same post, ch 3, (sc around post of next st, ch 3) 7 times; join in first sc.

Finish off and weave in all ends.

Layout

Row 9 — Row 8 — Row 7 — Row 6 — Row 5 — Row 4 — Row 3 — Row 2 — Row 1 —

Start border here

First Motif | Second Motif | Third Motif | Fourth Motif

Fifth Motif

Remaining Motifs
Referring to **Layout** for placement and motif color, work remaining motifs in same manner, joining on Rnd 12.

continued

Castle Grounds

Border

Hold afghan with right side facing you and one short end at top; join green in corner ch-7 sp at top of first motif in upper right-hand corner (see **Layout** on page 41).

Rnd 1:
Ch 4 **(counts as a dc and a ch-1 sp)**, in same sp work (dc, ch 1) 5 times; dc in same sp; † sc in next ch-3 sp, (ch 5, sk next ch-3 sp, sc in next ch-3 sp) 3 times; ch 3, sc in next ch-3 sp, (ch 5, sk next ch-3 sp, sc in next ch-3 sp) 3 times †; ch 1, sc in corner joining, ch 1; rep from † to † once; in next corner ch-7 sp work (dc, ch 1) 6 times; dc in same sp; †† rep from † to † once; ch 1, sc in corner joining, ch 1; rep from † to † once; in next corner ch-7 sp work (dc, ch 1) 6 times; dc in same sp ††; rep from †† to †† once more; working along next side, rep from † to † once; in next corner ch-7 sp work (dc, ch 1) 6 times; dc in same sp; rep from †† to †† 4 times; working along next side, rep from † to † once; in next corner ch-7 sp work (dc, ch 1) 6 times; dc in same sp; rep from †† to †† 3 times; working along next side, rep from † to † once; in next corner ch-7 sp work (dc, ch 1) 6 times; dc in same sp; rep from †† to †† 4 times; rep from † to † once; join in 3rd ch of beg ch-4.

Rnd 2:
Sl st in next ch-1 sp, ch 1, sc in same sp; (ch 3, sc in next ch-1 sp) 5 times; ch 3; † sc in next ch-5 sp, (ch 5, sc in next ch-5 sp) twice; in next ch-3 sp work (dc, ch 1) twice; dc in same sp; sc in next ch-5 sp, (ch 5, sc in next ch-5 sp) twice †; ch 2, keeping last lp of each dc on hook, dc in each of next 2 ch-1 sps, YO and draw through all 3 lps on hook; ch 2; rep from † to † once; (ch 3, sc in next ch-1 sp) 6 times; ch 3; †† rep from † to † once; ch 2, keeping last lp of each dc on hook, dc in each of next 2 ch-1 sps, YO and draw through all 3 lps on hook; rep from † to † once; (ch 3, sc in next ch-1 sp) 6 times; ch 3 ††; rep from †† to †† once more; working along next side, rep from † to † once; (ch 3, sc in next ch-1 sp) 6 times; ch 3; rep from †† to †† 4 times; working across next side, rep from † to † once; (ch 3, sc in next ch-1 sp) 6 times; ch 3; rep from †† to †† 3 times; working across next side, rep from † to † once; (ch 3, sc in next ch-1 sp) 6 times; ch 3; rep from †† to †† 4 times; rep from † to † once; ch 3; join in first sc.

Finish off and weave in all ends.

Day Lilies
designed by Eleanor Albano-Miles

These exotic flowers are added to the crocheted hexagon blocks like appliqués. We arranged the flowers in a circular pattern, but you might want to completely cover your afghan with lilies.

Day Lilies

Size:
About 51" x 70"

Materials:
Worsted weight yarn, 45 oz (3150 yds, 1350 gms) off white; 7 oz (490 yds, 210 gms) green; 4½ oz (315 yds, 135 gms) pink, orange, and gold

Note: *Our photographed afghan was made with Red Heart® Classic™, Off White #3, Seafoam Green #684, Pale Rose #755, Medium Coral #252, and Honey Gold #645.*

Size J (6mm) crochet hook, or size required for gauge
Size G (4.25mm) crochet hook
Size 16 tapestry needle

Gauge:
3 sc = 1"

Instructions

Motif (make 53)

With larger size hook and off white, ch 6; join to form a ring.

Rnd 1 (right side):
Ch 3 (counts as a dc on this and following rnd), 17 dc in ring; join in 3rd ch of beg ch-3—18 dc.

Rnd 2:
Ch 3, dc in same ch as joining; 2 dc in each rem dc; join in 3rd ch of beg ch-3—36 dc.

Note: *Remainder of motif is worked in joined rows.*

Row 1:
Ch 1, sc in same ch as joining and in next 4 dc, ch 3, sk next dc; * sc in next 5 dc, ch 3, sk next dc; rep from * 4 times more; join in first sc—6 ch-3 sps. Ch 3 (counts as first dc on following rows), turn.

Row 2:
In next ch-3 sp work (2 dc, ch 2, 2 dc); * dc in next 5 sc, in next ch-3 sp work (2 dc, ch 2, 2 dc); rep from * 4 times more; dc in next 4 dc; join in 3rd ch of turning ch-3—54 dc. Ch 3, turn.

Row 3:
Dc in next 6 dc, in next ch-2 sp work (dc, ch 2, dc); * dc in next 9 dc, in next ch-2 sp work (dc, ch 2, dc); rep from * 4 times more; dc in next 2 dc; join in 3rd ch of turning ch-3—66 dc. Ch 3, turn.

Row 4:
Dc in next 3 dc, in next ch-2 sp work (dc, ch 2, dc); * dc in next 11 dc, in next ch-2 sp work (dc, ch 2, dc); rep from * 4 times more; dc in next 7 dc; join in 3rd ch of turning ch-3—78 dc. Ch 1, turn.

Row 5:
Sc in same ch as joining and in next 8 dc, in next ch-2 sp work (sc, ch 2, sc); * sc in next 13 dc, in next ch-2 sp work (sc, ch 2, sc); rep from * 4 times more; sc in next 4 dc; join in first sc.

Finish off and weave in ends.

Lilies (make 10 pink, 10 orange, and 8 gold)

Top Half:
With smaller size hook, ch 4; join to form a ring.

Foundation Rnd (right side):
Ch 1, 9 sc in ring; join in BL of first sc.

FIRST PETAL:

Row 1:
Ch 1, 2 sc in same lp; working in BLs only, 2 sc in each of next 2 sc—6 sc. Ch 1, turn, leaving rem sc unworked.

Row 2:
Sc in first 2 sc, 2 sc in each of next 2 sc; sc in next 2 sc—8 sc. Ch 1, turn.

Row 3:
Sc in each sc. Ch 1, turn.

Row 4:
Rep Row 3.

Row 5:
Dec over first 2 sc (to work dec: draw up lp in 2 sc indicated, YO and draw through all 3 lps on hook—dec made); sc in next 4 sc, dec over next 2 sc—6 sc. Ch 1, turn.

Row 6:
Dec over first 2 sc; sc in next 2 sc, dec—4 sc. Ch 1, turn.

Rows 7 and 8:
Rep Row 3.

Row 9:
Dec twice—2 sc. Ch 1, turn.

Row 10:
Rep Row 3.

Row 11:
Dec. Ch 1, turn.

Row 12:
Sc in next sc. Finish off.

SECOND PETAL:
Join in BL of next unused sc on Foundation Rnd to left of First Petal.

Work same as First Petal.

THIRD PETAL:
Join in BL of next unused sc on Foundation Rnd to left of Second Petal.

Work same as First Petal.

Bottom Half:
Using smaller size hook, ch 4; join to form a ring.

Rnd 1 (right side):
Ch 1, 9 sc in ring; join in first sc.

Rnd 2:
Ch 3 (counts as a dc), dc in same sc; 2 dc in each rem sc; join in 3rd ch of beg ch-3—18 dc.

FIRST PETAL:

Row 1:
Ch 1, 2 sc in same ch as joining; working in BLs only, 2 sc in each of next 2 dc—6 sc. Ch 1, turn, leaving rem dc unworked.

Rows 2 through 12:
Rep Rows 2 through 12 of First Petal of Top Half.

SECOND PETAL:
Sk next 3 unused dc to left of First Petal; join in BL of next dc.

Work same as First Petal of Bottom Half.

THIRD PETAL:
Sk next 3 unused dc to left of Second Petal; join in BL of next dc.

Work same as Second Petal of Bottom Half.

Finish off and weave in all ends.

Leaf (make 168)
With smaller size hook and green, ch 12; sc in 2nd ch from hook, hdc in next ch, dc in next 2 chs, trc in next 3 chs, dc in next 2 chs, hdc in next ch, sc in next ch.

Finish off, leaving a 12" end for sewing.

Weave in rem end.

Lily Motif Assembly
Referring to **Photo A** for placement, sew six leaves to one motif. Referring to **Photo B**, sew bottom half of one lily to center of motif; tack end of each petal to Row 3 of motif. Referring to **Photo C**, sew matching top half over bottom half, positioning top half petals between petals of bottom half; tack end of each petal to Row 2 of motif. Repeat with remaining leaves and lilies.

Photo A

Photo B

Photo C

continued

Day Lilies

Afghan Assembly
Referring to **Layout** for placement, join motifs together. To join, hold two motifs with right sides together and carefully matching stitches. With tapestry needle and off white, sew with overcast stitch (see Stitch Guide on page 160) through BLs only along one side, beginning and ending in ch-2 sp of corners. Join remaining motifs in same manner, being sure all corner junctions are firmly joined.

Border
Hold afghan with right side facing you and one short end at top; with larger size hook, join green in ch-2 sp at top of first motif in upper right-hand corner (see **Layout**); ch 2, 2 hdc in same sp; hdc in next 15 sc, 3 hdc in next ch-2 sp; † (hdc in next 15 sc and in next joining) twice; (hdc in next 15 sc, 3 hdc in next ch-2 sp) twice †; rep from † to † twice more; hdc in next 15 sc; †† 3 hdc in next ch-2 sp; hdc in next 15 sc, in next joining, and in next 15 sc ††; rep from †† to †† 6 times more; (3 hdc in next ch-2 sp, hdc in next 15 sc) twice; 3 hdc in next ch-2 sp; rep from † to † 3 times; hdc in next 15 sc; rep from †† to †† 7 times; 3 hdc in next ch-2 sp; hdc in next 15 sc; join in 2nd ch of beg ch-2.

Finish off and weave in all ends.

Layout

Start border here

Parlor Bouquet
designed by Stephanie Hill

This afghan is as at home in a formal room as it would be in casual country surroundings. Popcorn stitches are used in the flowers and in the border for an interesting texture.

Parlor Bouquet

Size:
About 45" x 70"

Materials:
Worsted weight yarn, 36½ oz (2555 yds, 1095 gms) lt blue; 34 oz (2380 yds, 1020 gms) off white; 17 oz (1190 yds, 510 gms) pink

Note: *Our photographed afghan was made with Caron® Simply Soft®, Lt. Country Blue #9709, Off White #9702, and Plum Wine #9722.*

Size H (5mm) crochet hook, or size required for gauge
Size 16 tapestry needle

Gauge:
one motif = 6"

> ### Pattern Stitches
>
> **Beginning Popcorn (beg PC):**
> Ch 3, 3 dc in ring or sp indicated; drop lp from hook, insert hook in 3rd ch of beg ch-3, draw dropped lp through—beg PC made.
>
> **Popcorn (PC):**
> 4 dc in ring or sp indicated; drop lp from hook, insert hook in first dc made, draw dropped lp through—PC made.

Instructions

Motif (make 77)
With pink, ch 6; join to form a ring.

Rnd 1 (right side):
Beg PC (see Pattern Stitches) in ring; ch 3, [PC (see Pattern Stitches) in ring, ch 3] 3 times; join in top of beg PC—4 PCs.

Rnd 2:
Sl st in next ch-3 sp, in same sp work (beg PC, ch 3, PC)—beg corner made; ch 3; * in next ch-3 sp work (PC, ch 3, PC)—PC corner made; ch 3; rep from * twice more; join in top of beg PC. Finish off.

Rnd 3:
Join off white in any corner ch-3 sp; ch 3 (counts as a dc on this and following rnds), in same sp work (2 dc, ch 3, 3 dc)—beg dc corner made; 3 dc in next ch-3 sp; * in next corner ch-3 sp work (3 dc, ch 3, 3 dc)—dc corner made; 3 dc in next ch-3 sp; rep from * twice more; join in 3rd ch of beg ch-3.

Rnd 4:
Sl st in next 2 dc and in next ch-3 sp, beg dc corner in same sp; (3 dc in sp between next two 3-dc groups) twice; * in next corner ch-3 sp work dc corner; (3 dc in sp between next two 3-dc groups) twice; rep from * twice more; join in 3rd ch of beg ch-3. Finish off.

Rnd 5:
Join lt blue in any corner ch-3 sp; beg dc corner in same sp; (3 dc in sp between next two 3-dc groups) 3 times; * dc corner in next corner; (3 dc in sp between next two 3-dc groups) 3 times; rep from * twice more; join in 3rd ch of beg ch-3.

Rnd 6:
Sl st in next 2 dc and in next ch-3 sp, beg dc corner in same sp; (3 dc in sp between next two 3-dc groups) 4 times; * dc corner in next corner; (3 dc in sp between next two 3-dc groups) 4 times; rep from * twice more; join in 3rd ch of beg ch-3. Finish off.

Rnd 8:
Join off white in any corner ch-3 sp; ch 1, 3 sc in same sp—sc corner made; sc in next 18 dc; ***** 3 sc in next corner ch-3 sp—sc corner made; sc in next 18 dc; rep from ***** twice more; join in first sc.

Finish off and weave in all ends.

Assembly
Join motifs in 11 rows of 7 motifs each. To join motifs, hold 2 motifs with right sides together and carefully matching stitches; with tapestry needle and off white, sew with overcast stitch (see Stitch Guide on page 160) in BLs only along one side. Join motifs in rows and then sew rows together in same manner, being sure all 4-corner junctions are firmly joined.

Border
Hold afghan with right side facing you and one short end at top; join off white in 2nd sc of upper right-hand corner.

Rnd 1:
Ch 1, 3 sc in same sc—corner made; † sc in next 20 sc, hdc in next joining †; rep from † to † 5 times more; sc in next 20 sc, 3 sc in next sc—corner made; rep from † to † 10 times; sc in next 20 sc, 3 sc in next sc—corner made; rep from † to † 6 times; sc in next 20 sc, 3 sc in next sc—corner made; rep from † to † 10 times; sc in next 20 sc, join in first sc. Finish off.

Rnd 2:
Join rose in first sc of any 3-sc corner; in same sc work beg PC; ch 3, sk next st, PC in next sc—beg PC corner made; ***** sk next 2 sts, ch 3, † PC in next st; ch 3, sk next 2 sts †; rep from † to † to next corner; PC in first sc of corner, ch 3, sk next sc, PC in next sc—PC corner made; rep from ***** twice more; sk next 2 sts, ch 3; rep from † to † to next corner; join in beg PC. Finish off.

Rnd 3:
Join off white in any PC corner ch-3 sp; ch 3, in same sp work (2 dc, ch 3, 3 dc)—beg dc corner made; ***** 3 dc in each ch-3 sp to next PC corner ch-3 sp; in ch-3 sp work (3 dc, ch 3, 3 dc)—dc corner made; rep from ***** twice more; 3 dc in each ch-3 sp to beg ch-3; join in 3rd ch of beg ch-3. Finish off.

Rnd 4:
Join blue in any ch-3 corner sp; beg dc corner in same sp; ***** 3 dc in each sp between 3-dc groups to next dc corner ch-3 sp; in ch-3 sp work dc corner; rep from ***** twice more; 3 dc in each sp between 3-dc groups to beg ch-3; join in 3rd ch of beg ch-3.

Finish off and weave in ends.

Rose Dreams
designed by Nanette M. Seale

This feminine afghan reminds us of the romance of Victorian times. It is crocheted in panels, then the white leaves and spiral flowers are added for an elegant look.

Size:
About 49" x 63"

Materials:
Worsted weight yarn, 24 oz (1680 yds, 720 gms) white; 8 oz (560 yds, 240 gms) pink

Note: *Our photographed afghan was made with Red Heart® Super Saver, White #311 and Rose Pink #372.*

Size G (4.25mm) crochet hook, or size required for gauge
Size 16 tapestry needle

Gauge:
In pattern:
2 shells = 2½"
3 shell rows = 2"

Instructions

Panel (make 9)
With white, ch 188.

Rnd 1 (right side):
Dc in 4th ch from hook (beg 3 skipped chs count as a dc), ch 3, 2 dc in same ch as last dc made; * sk next 3 chs, in next ch work (2 dc, ch 3, 2 dc)—shell made; rep from * 45 times more; ch 3; working on opposite side in unused lps of beg ch, in lp at base of shell just made work (2 dc, ch 3, 2 dc)—shell made; † sk next 3 chs, in lp at base of next shell work (2 dc, ch 3, 2 dc)—shell made †; rep from † to † 45 times more; ch 3; join in 3rd ch of beg 3 skipped chs.

Rnd 2:
Sl st in next dc and in next ch-3 sp; ch 3 (counts as dc); in same sp work (dc, ch 3, 2 dc); *† in ch-3 sp of next shell work shell †; rep from * 45 times more; shell in next ch-3 sp; rep from † to † 47 times; shell in next ch-3 sp; join in 3rd ch of beg ch-3.

Rnd 3:
Sl st in next dc and in next ch-3 sp; ch 3, 4 dc in same sp; *† 5 dc in next ch-3 sp; rep from * 45 times more; sk next dc, 5 dc in sp between next 2 dc; 10 dc in next ch-3 sp; sk next dc, 5 dc in sp between next 2 dc †; 5 dc in next ch-3 sp; rep from † to † once; join in 3rd ch of beg ch-3. Finish off.

Rnd 4:
Join pink in first dc to left of joining; ch 2; working in BLs only, hdc in each st; join in 2nd ch of beg ch-2.

Finish off and weave in all ends.

continued

Rose Dreams

Assembly
Hold 2 panels with right sides together and long edges at top; with tapestry needle and pink, sew panels with overcast stitch (see Stitch Guide on page 160) through BLs only, beginning and ending 2" from top of panel. Repeat with remaining panels.

Border
Hold afghan with right side facing you and ends of panels at top; join white in 4th hdc from panel joining on 2nd panel from right.

Rnd 1 (right side):
Ch 3, in same hdc as joining work (dc, ch 3, 2 dc); * † sk next 3 hdc, shell in next hdc †; (sk next 2 hdc, shell in next hdc) 3 times; sk next 3 hdc on working panel, sk joining, sk first 3 hdc on next panel, shell in next hdc; rep from * 6 times more, then rep from † to † 67 times; †† sk next 3 hdc on working panel, sk joining, sk first 3 hdc on next panel, shell in next hdc; sk next 3 hdc, shell in next hdc; (sk next 2 hdc, shell in next hdc) 3 times ††; rep from †† to †† 6 times more; sk next 3 hdc on working panel, sk joining, sk first 3 hdc on next panel, shell in next hdc; rep from † to † 67 times; join in 3rd ch of beg ch-3, changing to pink by drawing lp through; cut white.

Rnd 2:
Sc in same st as joining and in next dc; * in next ch-3 sp work (2 sc, ch 3, sl st in 3rd ch from hook, sc); sc in next 4 dc; rep from * to last ch-3 sp; in last ch-3 sp work (2 sc, ch 3, sl st in 3rd ch from hook, sc); sc in next 2 dc; join in first sc.

Finish off and weave in all ends.

Rose (make 9)
With white, ch 37.

Row 1 (wrong side):
Sc in 2nd ch from hook; * ch 5, sk next 4 chs, sc in next ch; rep from * 6 times more—7 ch-5 sps. Turn.

Row 2 (right side):
In first ch-5 sp work (sl st, 5 sc, sl st)—small petal made; in next 2 lps work (sl st, 7 hdc, sl st)—medium petal made; in next 4 lps work (sl st, ch 2, 10 dc, sl st)—large petal made. Finish off.

Trim:
Hold piece with right side facing you; join pink in first sc of first small petal; sl st in each rem st and in each ch.
Finish off and weave in ends.

Leaf (make 9)
With white, ch 10.

Rnd 1 (right side):
3 dc in 4th ch from hook (beg 3 skipped chs count as a dc); dc in each ch to last ch; 7 dc in last ch; working on opposite side in unused lps of beg ch, dc in each lp to last lp; 3 dc in last lp; join in 3rd ch of beg 3 skipped chs.

Rnd 2:
Ch 1, sc in same ch as joining and in each dc to last 3 dc; ch 3, sl st in 3rd ch from hook, sc in last 3 dc; join in first sc.

Finish off and weave in ends.

Finishing:
Step 1:
To form rose, hold one rose with right side facing you, starting with first small petal, roll rose to right. With tapestry needle and matching yarn, tack in several places to hold shape. Repeat with remaining roses.

Step 2:
Tack one leaf to each rose.

Step 3:
Referring to photo for placement, with tapestry needle and white, sew roses to ends of every other panel (5 at top end and 4 at lower end).

Wedding Roses *designed by Ann Kirtley*

*S*ince roses are traditionally the symbol of love and romance, this filet crochet afghan is a wonderful choice as a wedding or anniversary gift. Its unusual ruffle border features roses in bloom for a lovely effect.

Wedding Roses

Size:
About 48" x 70"

Materials:
Worsted weight yarn, 65 oz (4550 yds, 1950 gms) off white

Note: Our photographed afghan was made with Red Heart® Classic™, Off White #3.

Size G (4.25mm) crochet hook, or size required for gauge
Size 16 tapestry needle

Gauge:
19 dc = 4"
9 rows = 4"

Instructions

Note: If you are not familiar with working filet from a chart, please read Filet Review on page 159.

Ch 195.

Row 1 (right side):
Dc in 4th ch from hook and in each rem ch—193 dc. Ch 3 (counts as first dc on following rows), turn.

Row 2:
Dc in next 3 dc; * † (ch 2, sk next 2 dc, dc in next dc) 20 times; dc in next 3 dc †; rep from * once more, then rep from † to † once; dc in next 2 dc and in 3rd ch of beg 3 skipped chs. Ch 3, turn.

Row 3:
Dc in next 3 dc; * † (ch 2, dc in next dc) 8 times; (2 dc in next ch-2 sp, dc in next dc) 6 times; (ch 2, dc in next dc) 6 times †; dc in next 3 dc; rep from * once more, then rep from † to † once; dc in next 2 dc and in 3rd ch of turning ch-3. Ch 3, turn.

Row 4:
Dc in next 3 dc; * † (ch 2, dc in next dc) 7 times; 2 dc in next ch-2 sp; dc in next 19 dc, (2 dc in next ch-2 sp, dc in next dc) twice; (ch 2, dc in next dc) 4 times †; dc in next 3 dc; rep from * once more, then rep from † to † once; dc in next 2 dc and in 3rd ch of turning ch-3. Ch 3, turn.

Following chart on page 55, work Rows 5 through 127.
At end of last row, do not ch 3. Finish off.

Edging

Hold afghan with right side facing you and Row 127 at top; join in 3rd ch of turning ch-3 in upper right-hand corner.

Rnd 1 (right side):
* Ch 4, dc in 4th ch from hook, sk next 2 dc, sl st in next dc; rep from * across; working along next side in edge dc and turning chs of rows, † ch 4, dc in 4th ch from hook, sl st in base of next row †; rep from † to † to beg ch; ch 4, dc in 4th ch from hook, working along lower edge in unused lps of beg ch, sl st in first lp; †† ch 4, dc in 4th ch from hook, sk next 2 lps, sl st in next lp ††; rep from †† to †† across; working along next side in edge dc and turning chs of rows, ch 4, dc in 4th ch from hook; sl st in Row 1; ††† ch 4, dc in 4th ch from hook, sl st in next row †††; rep from ††† to ††† to joining sl st; ch 4, dc in 4th ch from hook; join in joining sl st.

Rnd 2:
Sl st in next 2 chs of next ch-4 sp, ch 1, sc in same sp; ch 3; * sc in next ch-4 sp, ch 3; rep from * around; join in first sc.

Rnd 3:
Sl st in next ch-3 sp, ch 4 (counts as a trc), 10 trc in same sp; sk next ch-3 sp; * † (sl st in next sc and in next ch-3 sp) twice; turn; in same sp work (ch 3, sl st) 3 times; ch 1, turn, in ch-3 sp just made work (sc, hdc, 3 dc, hdc, sc)—small petal made; sl st in next sl st; † [in next ch-3 sp work (sc, hdc, 3 dc, hdc, sc)—small petal made; sl st in next sl st]; twice; sl st in next ch-3 sp on Rnd 2, turn; on working row (ch 5, working behind petals, sl st in back of next sl st) 3 times; on Rnd 2, sl st in next already worked ch-3 sp, ch 1, turn; [in next ch-5 sp work (sc, hdc, 5 dc, hdc, sc)—medium petal made; sl st in next sl st] 3 times; sl st in next sc on Rnd 2, turn; (ch 7, working behind petals, sl st in back of sl st behind next petal) 3 times; sl st in next sc, turn, [in next ch-7 sp work (sc, hdc, 7 dc, hdc, sc)—large petal made; sl st in next sl st] 3 times †; on Rnd 2, sk next ch-3 sp, 11 trc in next ch-3 sp; sk next ch-3 sp; rep from * 62 times more; then rep from † to † once; join in 4th ch of beg ch-4. Finish off.

Rnd 4:
Hold edging with right side facing you; working in BLs only, join in BL in 2nd dc on first large petal of Rnd 3; * † ch 7, sk next 3 dc, sl st in next dc, (ch 7, sl st in 2nd dc on next petal, ch 7, sk next 3 dc, sl st in next dc) twice; sl st in 4th trc of next 11-trc group, (ch 4, sl st in 4th ch from hook, sl st in next trc) 4 times †; sl st in 2nd dc of next petal; rep from * 62 times more, then rep from † to † once; join in joining sl st.

Finish off and weave in all ends.

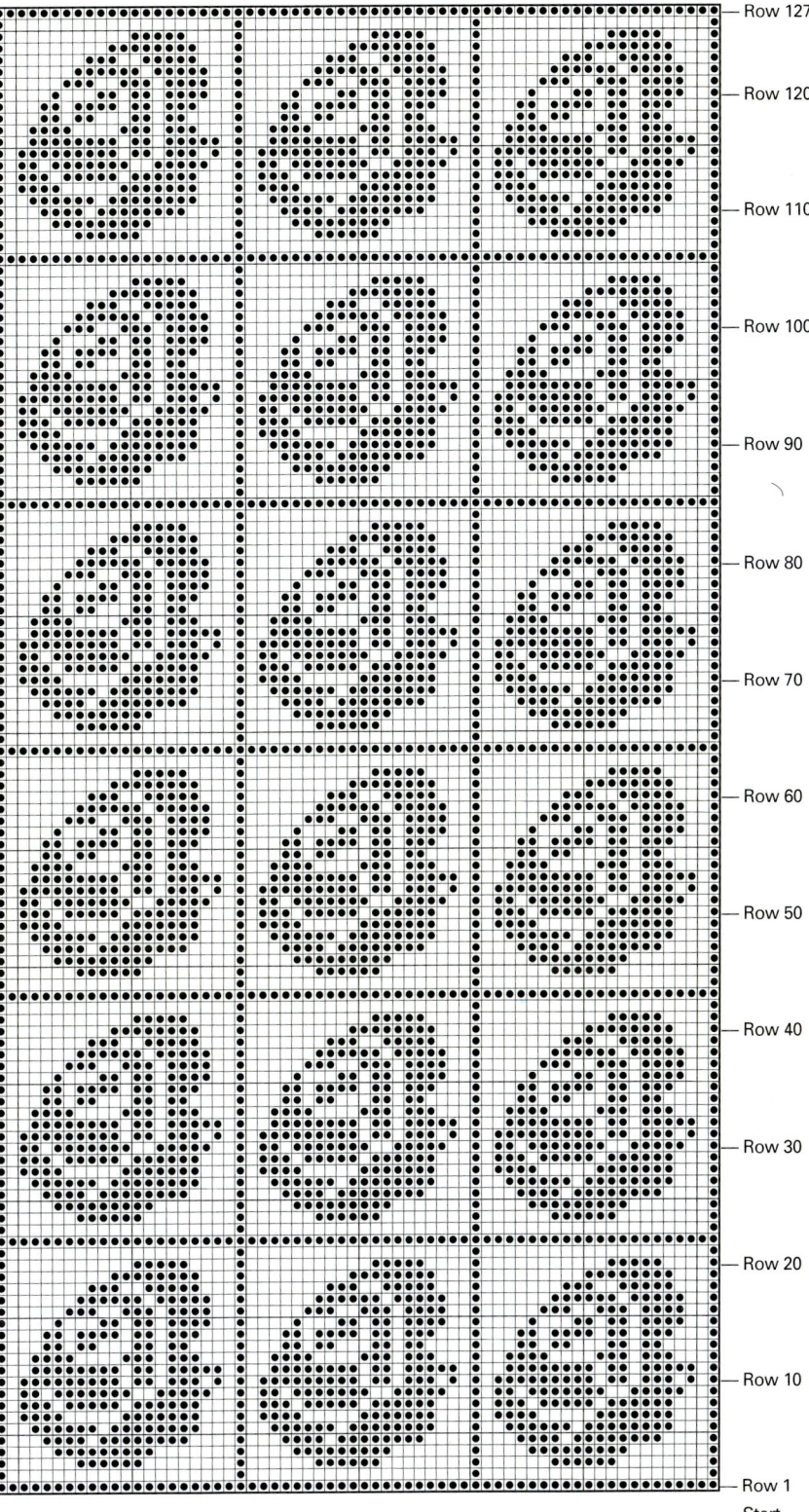

Wearing of the Green
designed by Diana Lynn Sippel

Size:
About 32" x 42"

Materials:
Worsted weight yarn, 11 oz (770 yds, 330 gms) each, lt green and dk green; 7 oz (490 yds, 210 gms) med green

Note: *Our photgraphed afghan was made with Coats and Clark® Classic, Spruce #362, Dark Spruce # 361, and Hunter Green #389.*

Size H (5mm) crochet hook, or size required for gauge
Size 16 tapestry needle

Gauge:
4 sc = 1"

Pattern Stitches

Front Post Half Double Crochet (FPhdc):
YO, insert hook from front to back to front around post (see Stitch Guide on page 160) of st indicated, YO and draw through all 3 lps on hook—FPhdc made.

Front Post Triple Crochet (FPtrc):
YO twice; insert hook from front to back to front around post (see Stitch Guide on page 160) of st indicated, (YO and draw through 2 lps on hook) 3 times—FPtrc made.

Long Half Double Crochet (long hdc):
YO, insert hook in sp indicated, YO and pull up lp to height of working rnd, YO and draw through all 3 lps on hook—long hdc made.

Instructions

Motif (make 48)
With lt green, ch 6; join to form a ring.

Rnd 1 (right side):
Ch 2, keeping last lp of each dc on hook, 2 dc in ring; YO and draw through all 3 lps on hook—beg cluster made; ch 1; keeping last lp of each dc on hook, 3 dc in ring; YO and draw through all 4 lps on hook—cluster made; ch 3; * cluster in ring; ch 1, cluster in ring; ch 3; rep from * twice more; join in top of first cluster. Change to med green by drawing lp through; cut lt green.

Rnd 2:
Ch 2 (counts as an hdc), hdc in next ch-1 sp and in next cluster; * 5 hdc in next ch-3 sp; hdc in next cluster, in next ch-1 sp, and in next cluster; rep from * twice more; 5 hdc in next ch-3 sp; join in 2nd ch of beg ch-2—32 hdc. Change to dk green by drawing lp through; cut med green.

This cozy throw will make you feel as if you are enjoying the luck of the Irish. It will keep you warm while reading a luxurious novel and sipping your favorite hot drink.

continued

Wearing of the Green

Rnd 3:
Ch 1; * FPhdc (see Pattern Stitches on page 57) around post of next cluster on 2nd rnd below; on working rnd, sk hdc behind FPhdc just made, sc in BL of next hdc, FPhdc around post of next cluster on 2nd rnd below; on working rnd, sk hdc behind FPhdc just made, sc in BLs of next 2 hdc, 3 sc in next hdc—corner made; sc in BLs of next 2 sc; rep from * 3 times more; join in first FPhdc.

Rnd 4:
Ch 1, sc in same FPhdc; * † sc in next sc, in next FPhdc, and in next 3 sc; 3 sc in next sc—corner made; sc in next 3 sc †; sc in next FPhdc; rep from * twice more, then rep from † to † once; join in first sc—48 sc. Change to lt green; cut dk green.

Rnd 5:
Ch 1, sc in same sc; FPtrc (see Pattern Stitches on page 57) around post of next hdc (between FPhdc) on 2nd rnd below; * † sk next sc, sc in next 5 sc, 3 long hdc (see Pattern Stitches on page 57) in next ch-3 sp on 2nd rnd below; on working rnd, sk next sc (behind 3 long hdc just made) †; sc in next 5 sc, FPtrc around next hdc; rep from * twice more, then rep from † to † once; sc in next 4 sc; join in first sc.

Finish off and weave in all ends.

Assembly
Join motifs in 8 rows of 6 motifs each. To join, hold 2 motifs with right sides together and carefully matching stitches; with tapestry needle and lt green, sew together with overcast stitch (see Stitch Guide on page 160) through BLs only along one side. Join motifs in rows and then sew rows in same manner, being sure all four-corner junctions are firmly joined.

Border
Hold afghan with right side facing you and one short end at top; join dk green in upper right-hand corner in 2nd long hdc of 3-hdc group.

Rnd 1 (right side):
Ch 2, 2 hdc in same st as joining—corner made; * hdc in each st to next corner; 3 hdc in next corner—corner made; rep from * twice more; sc in each st to first sc; join in 2nd ch of beg ch-2. Change to lt green by drawing lp through.

Rnd 2:
Ch 1, sc in same ch as joining; 3 sc in next hdc—corner made; * sc in each hdc to 2nd hdc of next corner; 3 sc in 2nd hdc; rep from * twice more; sc in each sc to first sc; join in first sc. Change to dk green by drawing lp through; cut lt green.

Rnd 3:
Ch 3, sk first 2 sc; * sl st in next sc, ch 3, sk next sc; rep from * around; join in 3rd ch of beg ch-3.

Finish off and weave in all ends.

Out of the Ordinary

*F*or those who are always looking for something new to try, this is the section for you. There are afghans with a second layer of surface decoration, innovative squares and even one that reverses.

- **A Little Bit of Chocolate . 60**
- **Antique Lace 63**
- **Baltic Tiles 66**
- **Blue Lagoon 69**
- **Flower Power 72**
- **Lollipop Confection 75**
- **Old Cathedral 79**
- **Simply Scrumptious 82**

A Little Bit of Chocolate
designed by Diana Lynn Sippel

Size:
About 38" x 50"

Materials:
Worsted weight yarn, 18 oz (1260 yds, 540 gms) brown; 12 oz (840 yds, 360 gms) each, tan and beige

Note: *Our photographed afghan was made with Red Heart® Super Saver, Brown #328, Warm Brown #336, and Buff #334.*

Size G (4.25mm) crochet hook, or size required for gauge
Size 16 tapestry needle

Gauge:
4 sc = 1"

Pattern Stitches

Long Double Crochet (long dc):
YO, insert hook in sp indicated, draw up lp to height of working rnd, (YO, draw through 2 lps on hook) twice—long dc made.

Front Post Double Crochet (FPdc):
YO, insert hook from front to back to front around posts (see Stitch Guide on page 160) of 2 sts indicated at the same time, draw up lp; (YO and draw through 2 lps on hook) twice—FPdc made.

Instructions

Note: *To change colors in a joining sl st, with new color draw up lp in joining st and draw through remaining lp on hook. Cut old color, unless otherwise specified.*

Hexagon (make 53)
With beige, ch 5; join to form a ring.

Rnd 1 (right side):
Ch 4 (counts as a trc), 23 trc in ring; join in BL of 4th ch of beg ch-4, changing to brown in joining.

Note: *FPdc on following rnd is worked around 2 sts indicated at same time.*

Rnd 2:
Ch 1, sc in same lp as joining; FPdc (see Pattern Stitches) around post of beg ch 4 of Rnd 1 and post of next trc; * on working rnd, sc in BLs of next 2 trc, FPdc around post of last trc worked and post of next trc; rep from * 10 times more; join in first sc, changing to tan—36 sts. Drop brown; do not cut.

Rnd 3:
Ch 1, sc in same sc; * sc in next FPdc, dc in unused lps of next 2 trc on Rnd 1; rep from * 11 times more; join in BL of first sc, changing to brown. Cut tan.

continued

Making this afghan is like eating a chocolate bar—you do it one piece at a time. This unique hexagon motif is created with post stitches around the center and has long stitches in each corner that when joined to other hexagons form a secondary pattern.

A Little Bit of Chocolate

Rnd 4:
Ch 1, sc in same sc; * FPdc around next FPdc on 2nd rnd below; on working rnd, sc in BLs of next 3 sts; rep from * 10 times more; FPdc around next FPdc on 2nd rnd below; on working row, sc in BLs of next 2 sts; join in BL of first sc.

Rnd 5:
Ch 1, sc in same sc, 3 sc in BL of next st; * working in BLs only, sc in next 7 sts, 3 sc in next st; rep from * 4 times more; sc in next 6 sts; join in BL of first sc, changing to beige in joining. Cut brown.

Note: On following rnd, sk only 1 st behind each 3-long dc group.

Rnd 6:
Ch 1, sc in same lp as joining and in BL of next sc; * † working over next 3-sc group on Rnd 5, 3 long dc (see Pattern Stitches on page 61) in same lp on Rnd 4 as 3 sc made †; sc in BLs of next 9 sts; rep from * 4 times more, then rep from † to † once; sc in BLs of next 7 sts; join in first sc.

Assembly
Referring to **Layout** for placement, join motifs together in 4 rows of 8 motifs and 3 rows of 7 motifs. To join, hold two motifs with right sides together and carefully matching stitches; with tapestry needle and beige, sew together with overcast stitch (see Stitch Guide on page 160) through BLs only along one side, beginning and ending with 2nd long dc of 3-long dc groups. Join remaining motifs in same manner, alternating rows of 8 motifs with rows of 7 motifs, and being sure all corner junctions are firmly joined.

Border
Hold afghan with right side facing you and one short end at top; join brown in 2nd long dc of point in upper right-hand corner (see **Layout**).

Rnd 1 (right side):
Ch 1, 3 sc in same st as joining; sc in next 11 sts, 3 sc in next long dc; * sc in next 10 sts; † draw up lp in next long dc, in next joining, and in next long dc, YO and draw through all 4 lps on hook †; sc in next 9 sts; rep from † to † once; sc in next 10 sts, 3 sc in next long dc; sc in next 11 sts, 3 sc in next long dc; rep from * twice more; sc in next 11 sts, 3 sc in next long dc; †† sc in next 10 sts, rep

Layout

from † to † once; sc in next 10 sts, 3 sc in next long dc ††; rep from †† to †† 6 times more; (sc in next 11 sts, 3 sc in next long dc) twice; sc in next 10 sts; rep from † to † once; sc in next 9 sts; rep from † to † once; sc in next 10 sts, 3 sc in next long dc; sc in next 11 sts, 3 sc in next long dc; sc in next 10 sts, rep from † to † once; sc in next 9 sts; rep from † to † once; sc in next 10 sts, 3 sc in next long dc; sc in next 11 sts, 3 sc in next long dc; sc in next 10 sts; rep from † to † once; sc in next 9 sts; rep from † to † once; sc in next 10 sts, 3 sc in next long dc; sc in next 11 sts, 3 sc in next long dc; rep from †† to †† 7 times; sc in next 11 sts; join in first sc.

Rnd 2:
Ch 1, sc in same sc and in each rem sc; join in first sc. Finish off and weave in all ends.

Antique Lace *designed by Eleanor Albano-Miles*

The beautiful crochet stitches in the lacy squares of this afghan show up beautifully when they are joined to the single crochet squares beneath them.

Antique Lace

Size:
About 48" x 60"

Materials:
Worsted weight yarn, 46½ oz (3255 yds, 1395 gms) off white; 26 oz (1820 yds, 780 gms) beige

Note: Our photographed afghan was made with Red Heart® Soft, New Aran #7313 and Lt Wheat #7320.

Size J (6mm) crochet hook, or size required for gauge
Size 16 tapestry needle

Gauge:
7 sc = 2"

Pattern Stitches

Cluster (CL):
Keeping last lp of each trc on hook, 3 trc in sp indicated, YO and draw through all 4 lps on hook—CL made.

Double Crochet Cluster (dcCL):
Keeping last lp of each dc on hook, 3 dc in st indicated; YO and draw through all 4 lps on hook—dcCL made.

Double Triple Crochet (dtrc):
YO 3 times, draw up lp in st or sp indicated, (YO, draw through 2 lps on hook) 4 times—dtrc made.

Three-Double Triple Crochet Cluster (3-dtrc CL):
Keeping last lp of each dtrc on hook, 3 dtrc in st or sp indicated, YO and draw through all 4 lps on hook—3-dtrc CL made.

Four-Double Triple Crochet Cluster (4-dtrc CL):
Keeping last lp of each dtrc on hook, 4 dtrc in st or sp indicated, YO and draw through all 5 lps on hook—4-dtrc CL made.

Long Single Crochet (long sc):
Insert hook in corresponding sc on 2nd rnd below, draw up lp to working rnd, YO and draw through 2 lps on hook—long sc made.

Instructions

Lace Motif (make 20)
With beige, ch 9; join to form a ring.

Rnd 1 (right side):
Ch 1, 24 sc in ring; join in first sc.

Rnd 2:
Ch 6, 3-dtrc CL (see Pattern Stitches) over next 3 sc; * ch 7, 4-dtrc CL (see Pattern Stitches) over same sc as last dtrc of 3-dtrc CL just made and next 3 sc; rep from * 5 times more; ch 7, 4-dtrc CL over same sc as last dc of last 4-dtrc CL made, next 2 sc, and same sc as beg ch-6; join in first 3-dtrc CL—8 clusters.

Rnd 3:
Ch 1, sc in same cluster; ch 3, in next ch-7 sp work (sc, ch 3) 3 times; * sc in next cluster, ch 3, in next ch-7 sp work (sc, ch 3) 3 times; rep from * 6 times more; join in first sc.

Rnd 4:
Sl st in next ch-3 sp, ch 1, sc in same sp; ch 3; * sc in next ch-3 sp, ch 3; rep from * around; join in first sc.

Rnd 5:
Rep Rnd 4.

Rnd 6:
Sl st in next ch-3 sp, ch 1, sc in same sp; ch 3, (sc in next ch-3 sp, ch 3) 4 times; sk next ch-3 sp; *† in next ch-3 sp work [CL (see Pattern Stitches), ch 5, 4-dtrc CL, ch 5, CL]; ch 3 †; sk next ch-3 sp, (sc in next ch-3 sp, ch 3) 5 times; sk next ch-3 sp; rep from * twice more, then rep from † to † once; join in first sc. Finish off.

Rnd 7:
Join beige in any 4-dtrc CL; ch 1, in same sp work (sc, ch 2, sc)—corner made; 2 sc in next ch-5 sp; sc in next st, (2 sc in next ch-3 sp, sc in next st) 6 times; 2 sc in next ch-5 sp; * in next 4-dtrc CL work (sc, ch 2, sc)—corner made; 2 sc in next ch-5 sp; sc in next st, (2 sc in next ch-3 sp, sc in next st) 6 times; 2 sc in next ch-5 sp; rep from * twice more; join in first sc.

Finish off and weave in ends.

Solid Square (make 20)
With off white, ch 35.

Row 1 (wrong side):
Sc in 2nd ch from hook and in each rem ch—34 sc. Ch 1, turn.

Row 2 (right side):
Sc in each sc. Ch 1, turn.

Rows 3 through 37:
Rep Row 2.

Edging:
In first sc work corner; sk next sc, (sc in next 3 sc, sk next sc) 7 times; sk next sc, sc in next 2 sc, sk next sc, in next sc work corner; working along next side in edge sc, † sk next row (sc in next row, sk next row) twice; (sc in next 2 rows, sk next row) 3 times; (sc in next 3 rows, sk next row, sc in next row, sk next row, sc in next 3 rows, sk next row, (sc in next 2 rows, sk next row) 3 times; (sc in next row, sk next row) twice †; working along lower edge in unused lps of beg ch, in first lp work corner; sk next lp, (sc in next 3 lps, sk next lp) 7 times; sk next lp, sc in next 2 lps, sk next lp, in next lp work corner; working along next side in edge sc; rep from † to † once; join in first sc.

Finish off and weave in ends.

Joining
Place wrong side of one lace motif facing right side of one solid square, carefully matching corners; join white through both thicknesses in any corner ch-2 sp.

Rnd 1:
Ch 1, working through both thicknesses, corner in same sp; sc in each sc to next corner ch-2 sp; * corner in ch-2 sp; sc in each sc to next corner ch-2 sp; rep from * once more; sc in each sc to first sc; join in first sc. Finish off.

Rnd 2:
Join off white in any corner ch-2 sp; corner in same sp; sc in each sc to next corner ch-2 sp; * corner in ch-2 sp; sc in each sc to next corner ch-2 sp; rep from * twice more; join in first sc.

Rnd 3:
Ch 1, sc in same sc as joining; * corner in next ch-2 sp; sc in each sc to next corner ch-2 sp; rep from * twice more; corner in next ch-2 sp; sc in each sc to first sc; join in first sc. Finish off.

Rnd 4:
Hold joined motif with wrong side facing you; join beige in any corner ch-2 sp; ch 1, corner in same sp; *† sc in next sc, trc in next sc, [sc in next sc, dcCL (see Pattern Stitches) in next sc, sc in next sc, trc in next sc] 7 times; sc in next sc †; corner in next ch-2 sp; rep from * twice more, then rep from † to † once; join in first sc. Finish off.

Rnd 5:
Hold joined motif with right side facing you; join off white in any corner ch-2 sp; ch 1, corner in same sp; long sc (see Pattern Stitches) in corresponding ch-2 sp on 2nd rnd below; *† (long sc in next sc on 2nd rnd below, sc in next st) 15 times; long sc in next sc on 2nd rnd below; long sc in corner ch-2 sp on 2nd rnd below †; corner in next ch-2 sp; long sc in same ch-2 sp on 2nd rnd below; rep from * twice more, then rep from † to † once; join in first sc. Ch 1, turn.

Note: Remainder of joining is worked as joined rows.

Row 1:
* Sc in each sc to next corner ch-2 sp; corner in ch-2 sp; rep from * 3 times more; join in first sc. Ch 1, turn.

Row 2:
Rep Row 1. At end of rnd, do not ch 1.

Finish off and weave in all ends.

Join rem lace motifs to solid squares in same manner.

Assembly
Join squares in 5 rows of 4 squares each. To join squares, hold 2 squares with right sides together and carefully matching stitches; with tapestry needle and off white, sew with overcast stitch (see Stitch Guide on page 160) through BLs only along one side. Join squares in rows, then sew rows together in same manner, making sure all four-corner junctions are firmly joined.

Border
Hold afghan with right side facing you and one short end at top; join off white in ch-2 sp in upper right-hand corner, ch 1, 3 sc in same sp; † sc in each st to next joined ch-2 sp, sc in joined ch-2 sp, hdc in joining, sc in next joined ch-2 sp †; rep from † to † twice more; sc in each st to next corner ch-2 sp; 3 sc in corner ch-2 sp; rep from † to † 4 times; sc in each st to next corner ch-2 sp; 3 sc in corner ch-2 sp; rep from † to † 3 times; sc in each st to next corner ch-2 sp; 3 sc in corner ch-2 sp; rep from † to † 4 times; sc in each st to first sc; join in first sc.

Finish off and weave in ends.

Baltic Tiles *designed by Mary Lamb Becker*

Size:
About 45" x 60"

Materials:
Worsted weight yarn, 31 oz (2170 yds, 930 gms) blue;
  10 oz (700 yds, 300 gms) yellow;
  14 oz (980 yds, 420 gms) off white

Note: *Our photographed afghan was made with Red Heart® Classic™, True Blue #822, Honey Gold #645, and Off White #3.*

Size I (5.5mm) crochet hook, or size required for gauge
Size 16 tapestry needle

Gauge:
3 sc = 1"

Pattern Stitch

Double Triple Crochet (dtrc):
YO 3 times, draw up lp in st or sp indicated, (YO, draw through 2 lps on hook) 4 times—dtrc made.

Instructions

Square (make 35)
With off white, ch 4; join to form a ring.

Rnd 1 (right side):
Ch 6 (counts as a dc and a ch-3 sp), (3 dc in ring, ch 3) 3 times; 2 dc in ring; join in 3rd ch of beg ch-6—4 ch-3 sps.

Rnd 2:
Sl st in next ch-3 sp; ch 3, in same sp work (dc, ch 3, 2 dc)—beg corner made; * sk next dc, in next dc work (trc, dc, trc); in next ch-3 sp work (2 dc, ch 3, 2 dc)—corner made; rep from * twice more; sk next dc, in next dc work (trc, dc, trc); join in 3rd ch of beg ch-3. Finish off.

Rnd 3:
With yellow make slip knot on hook and join with an sc in any corner ch-3 sp; in same sp work (sc, ch 3, 2 sc); * † sc in next dc, sk next dc, 2 dc in next trc; ch 3, sk next dc, 2 dc in next trc; sk next dc, sc in next dc †; in next corner ch-3 sp work (2 sc, ch 3, 2 sc); rep from * twice more, then rep from † to † once; join in first sc. Finish off.

Who said a granny couldn't be innovative and elegant? This granny square done in blue, white and gold has the look of beautiful ceramic tiles.

continued

Baltic Tiles

Rnd 4:
Working behind Rnd 3, join off white in any corner ch-3 sp on Rnd 2 between 2-sc groups of Rnd 3; ch 4 (counts as a dc and a ch-1 sp on this and following rnds), dc in same sp—beg corner made; * † 3 dc in next skipped dc; in next skipped dc work (dc, ch 1, dc)—corner made; 3 dc in next skipped dc †; in next corner ch-3 sp between 2-sc groups work (dc, ch 1, dc); rep from * twice more, then rep from † to † once; join in 3rd ch of beg ch-4.

Rnd 5:
Sl st in next corner ch-1 sp, ch 4, dc in same sp—beg corner made; * † dc in next 3 sts, hdc in next st, sk next st, 3 sc in next ch-1 sp; sk next st, hdc in next st, dc in next 3 sts †; in next corner ch-1 sp work (dc, ch 1, dc)—corner made; rep from * twice more, then rep from † to † once; join in 3rd ch of beg ch-4. Finish off.

Rnd 6:
With blue make slip knot on hook and join with an sc in any corner ch-1 sp; dtrc (see Pattern Stitch on page 67) in next ch-3 sp on Rnd 3; on working rnd, sc in same corner—corner made; * † sc in next 4 sts, trc in next ch-3 sp on Rnd 3; in same sp work (2 dc, trc); on working rnd, sk next 5 sts, sc in next 4 sts †; sc in next corner ch-1 sp, dtrc in next ch-3 sp on Rnd 3; on working rnd, sc in same sp—corner made; rep from * twice more, then rep from † to † once; join in first sc.

Rnd 7:
Sl st in next dtrc, ch 4 (counts as first dc and ch-1 sp), dc in same dtrc—beg corner made; * † dc in next 5 sc; on Rnd 5, sk next unworked hdc and sc, 3 dc in next sc; on working rnd, sk next trc, next 2 dc, and next trc, dc in next 5 sc †; in next dtrc work (dc, ch 1, dc)—corner made; rep from * twice more, then rep from † to † once; join in 3rd ch of beg ch-4. Finish off.

Rnd 8:
With yellow make slip knot on hook and join with an sc in any corner, ch 5, sc in same sp—beg corner made; * † sc in next 5 sts, sk next st, in next st work (dc, trc); ch 3, sk next st, in next st work (trc, dc); sk next st, sc in next 5 sts †; in next corner work (sc, ch 5, sc)—corner made; rep from * twice more, then rep from † to † once; join in first sc. Finish off.

Rnd 9:
With blue make slip knot on hook and join with an sc in any corner; in same sp work (sc, ch 1, 2 sc)—beg corner made; * † dc in next 6 sc, sk next dc and next trc, working behind ch-3 sp, in next skipped st on Rnd 7 work (trc, ch 1, dc, ch 1, trc); on working rnd, sk next trc and next dc, dc in next 6 sc †; in next corner work (2 sc, ch 1, 2 sc)—corner made; rep from * twice more, then rep from † to † once; join in first sc.

Rnd 10:
Sl st in next sc and in next ch-1 sp, ch 4, dc in same sp—beg corner made; * † dc in each st and in each ch-1 sp to next corner ch-1 sp †; in corner ch-1 sp work (dc, ch 1, dc)—corner made; rep from * twice more, then rep from † to † once; join in 3rd ch of beg ch-4.

Finish off and weave in all ends.

Assembly

Join squares in 7 rows of 5 squares each. To join squares, hold two squares with right sides together and carefully matching stitches; with tapestry needle and blue, sew with overcast stitch (see Stitch Guide on page 160) through BLs only along one side, beginning and ending with corner ch-1 sp. Join squares in rows; then join rows together in same manner, being sure that all four-corner junctions are firmly joined.

Edging

Hold afghan with right side facing you and one short end at top; join blue in ch-1 sp in upper right-hand corner.

Rnd 1:
Ch 1, 3 sc in same sp—corner made; working in BLs only, † sc in each dc to next joining; hdc in joining †; rep from † to † 3 times more; sc in each dc to next corner ch-1 sp; 3 sc in corner ch-1 sp—corner made; rep from † to † 6 times; sc in each dc to next corner ch-1 sp; 3 sc in corner ch-1 sp—corner made; rep from † to † 4 times; sc in each dc to next corner ch-1 sp; 3 sc in corner ch-1 sp—corner made; rep from † to † 6 times; sc in each dc to first sc; working through both lps join in first sc.

Rnd 2:
Ch 1, sc in same sc as joining; * 3 sc in next sc; sc in each sc to 2nd sc of next corner; rep from * twice more; 3 sc in next sc; sc in each sc to first sc; join in first sc.

Finish off and weave in ends.

Blue Lagoon
designed by Eleanor Albano-Miles

The clever idea of placing a very lacy square on top of a solid square allows us to enjoy this original pattern.

Blue Lagoon

Size:
About 48" x 62"

Materials:
Worsted weight yarn, 60 oz (4200 yds, 1800 gms) white; 3 oz (210 yds, 90 gms) each, lt blue, lt med blue, med blue, dk med blue, and dk blue

Note: Our photographed afghan was made with Red Heart® Classic™ White #001, Jewel Blue #818; Super Saver, Lt Periwinkle #347, True Blue #822, Skipper Blue #848, and Olympic Blue #849.

Size J (6mm) crochet hook, or size required for gauge
Size 16 tapestry needle

Gauge:
7 sc = 2"
4 sc rows = 1"

Instructions

Lace Motif (make 20)
With lt blue, ch 8; join to form a ring.

Rnd 1 (right side):
Ch 8, sl st in 6th ch from hook (5 skipped chs count as a ch-5 sp; * 4 dc in ring; ch 5, sl st in last dc made; rep from * 6 times more; 3 dc in ring; join in 3rd ch of beg ch-8. Finish off.

Rnd 2:
Hold piece with right side facing you; join lt med blue in any ch-5 sp; ch 3 (counts as a dc on this and following rnds), in same sp work (dc, ch 2, 2 dc)—beg shell made; ch 2; * in next ch-5 sp work (2 dc, ch 2, 2 dc)—shell made; ch 2; rep from * 6 times more; join in 3rd ch of beg ch-3. Finish off.

Rnd 3:
Hold piece with right side facing you; join med blue in ch-2 sp of any shell; beg shell in same sp; ch 4; * in ch-2 sp of next shell work shell; ch 4; rep from * 6 times more; join in 3rd ch of beg ch-3. Finish off.

Rnd 4:
Hold piece with right side facing you; join dk med blue in ch-2 sp of any shell; beg shell in same sp; ch 6; * shell in next shell; ch 6; rep from * 6 times more; join in 3rd ch of beg ch-3. Finish off.

Rnd 5:
Hold piece with right side facing you; join dk blue in ch-2 sp of any shell; beg shell in same sp; ch 8; * shell in next shell; ch 8; rep from * 6 times more; join in 3rd ch of beg ch-3. Finish off.

Rnd 6:
Hold piece with right side facing you; join white in ch-2 sp of any shell, ch 1, sc in same sp; * † ch 10, sc in next ch-2 sp, ch 20 †; sc in next ch-2 sp; rep from * twice more, then rep from † to † once; join in first sc.

Rnd 7:
Ch 1, sc in same sc; * † 10 sc in next ch-10 sp; sc in next sc, in next ch-20 sp work (11 sc, ch 2, 11 sc) †; sc in next sc; rep from * twice more, then rep from † to † once; join in first sc.

Finish off and weave in all ends.

Solid Square (make 20)
With white, ch 35.

Row 1 (right side):
Sc in 2nd ch from hook and in each rem ch—34 sc. Ch 1, turn.

Row 2:
Sc in each sc. Ch 1, turn.

Rows 3 through 42:
Rep Row 2.

Edging:
In first sc work (sc, ch 2, sc)—corner made; sc in next 32 sc, in next sc work (sc, ch 2, sc)—corner made; † working along next side in ends of rows, (sk next row, sc in next 4 rows) 8 times; sk next row †; working across next side in unused lps of beg ch, in next lp work (sc, ch 2, sc)—corner made; sc in next 32 lps, in next lp work (sc, ch 2, sc)—corner made; rep from † to † once; join in first sc. Finish off.

Joining
Place wrong side of one lace motif facing right side of one solid square, carefully matching corners; join white through both thicknesses in any corner ch-2 sp.

Note: Joining is worked in joined rows.

Row 1 (right side):
Ch 1, in same sp work (sc, ch 2, sc)—corner made; working through both thicknesses, * † sc in each sc to next corner ch-2 sp; in corner ch-2 sp work (sc, ch 2, sc)—corner made; rep from * twice more, then rep from † to † once; join in first sc. Ch 3 (counts as first dc on following row), turn.

Row 2:
* Dc in each sc to next corner ch-2 sp; in corner sp work (dc, ch 2, dc)—corner made; rep from * 3 times more; join in 3rd ch of turning ch-3. Ch 1, turn.

Row 3:
Sc in same ch as joining and in next dc; * † in corner ch-2 sp work (sc, ch 2, sc)—corner made †; sc in each dc to next corner ch-2 sp; rep from * twice more, then rep from † to † once; sc in each sc to first sc; join in first sc.

Finish off and weave in all ends.

Assembly
Join squares in 5 rows of 4 squares each. To join squares, hold 2 squares with right sides together and carefully matching stitches; with tapestry needle and white, sew with overcast stitch (see Stitch Guide on page 160) through BLs only along one side. Join squares in rows; then sew rows together in same manner, making sure all four-corner junctions are firmly joined.

Border
Hold afghan with right side facing you and one short end at top; with white make slip knot on hook and join with an sc in ch-2 sp in upper right-hand corner; 2 sc in same sp; working in BLs only, † sc in next 41 sts, hdc in joining †; rep from † to † twice more; †† sc in next 41 sts, 3 sc in next corner ch-2 sp ††; rep from † to † 4 times; rep from †† to †† once; rep from † to † 3 times; rep from †† to †† once; rep from † to † 4 times; sc in next 41 sts, join in joining sc.

Finish off and weave in ends.

Flower Power
designed by Diana Lynn Sippel

Not only is this a wonderful, innovative afghan, it's also an excellent way to use up all your scraps of yarn leftover from other projects.

Size:
About 44" x 58"

Materials:
Worsted weight yarn, 20 oz (1400 yds, 600 gms) black; 3 oz (210 yds, 90 gms) yellow; 14 oz (980 yds, 420 gms) scraps

Note: Our photographed afghan was made with Red Heart® Soft, Black #7012, Bright Yellow #7231, and less than one skein each of 13 different colors.

Size F (3.75mm) crochet hook, or size required for gauge
Size 16 tapestry needle

Gauge:
one hexagon = 5½" point to point

Pattern Stitch

Front Post Double Crochet (FPdc):
YO, insert hook from front to back to front around posts (see Stitch Guide on page 160) of 2 sts indicated at the same time, draw up lp, (YO, draw through 2 lps on hook) twice—FPdc made.

Instructions

Hexagons (make 86)
With yellow, ch 4; join to form a ring.

Rnd 1 (right side):
Ch 3 (counts as a dc), dc in ring, ch 2, (2 dc in ring, ch 2) 5 times; join in 3rd ch of beg ch-3. Change to any scrap color by drawing lp through; cut old color.

Rnd 2:
Ch 1, sc in same ch as joining; sc in next dc, 3 sc in next ch-2 sp; * sc in next 2 dc, 3 sc in next ch-3 sp; rep from * 4 times more; join in first sc.

Rnd 3:
Ch 1, sc in same sc and in next sc; sk next sc, 5 dc in next sc; sk next sc; * sc in next 2 sc, sk next sc, 5 dc in next sc; sk next sc; rep from * 4 times more; join in first sc. Change to new scrap color by drawing lp through; cut old color.

Note: Always work FPdc around both posts at same time.

Rnd 4:
Ch 1; * FPdc (see Pattern Stitch) around next 2 dc on 3rd rnd below; on working rnd, sk next 2 sc behind FPdc; sc in next dc, 2 sc in each of next 3 dc; sc in next dc; rep from * 5 times more; join in first FPdc. Change to black by drawing lp through; cut old color.

continued

Flower Power

Rnd 5:
Ch 2 **(counts as an hdc)**; * † hdc in next 2 sc, sc in next sc, 2 sc in each of next 2 sc; sc in next sc, hdc in next 2 sc †; hdc in next FPdc, rep from * 4 times more, then rep from † to † once; join in 2nd ch of beg ch-2.

Rnd 6:
Ch 1, sc in same ch as joining and in next 5 sts; * 3 sc in next st; sc in next 10 sts; rep from * 4 times more; 3 sc in next st; sc in next 4 sts; join in first sc.

Finish off and weave in all ends.

Assembly

Referring to **Layout** for placement, join hexagons together in 5 rows of 10 hexagons and 4 rows of 9 hexagons. To join, hold two hexagons with right sides together and carefully matching stitches; with tapestry needle and black, sew together with overcast stitch **(see Stitch Guide on page 160)** through BLs only along one side, beginning and ending with corner sc. Join hexagons in rows. Sew rows together in same manner alternating 10 hexagon rows with 9 hexagon rows.

Border

Hold afghan with one short end at top; join black in 2nd sc of upper right-hand corner (see **Layout**).

Rnd 1 (right side):
Ch 3 **(counts as an hdc and a ch-1 sp)**, sk next sc; * hdc in next sc, ch 1, sk next sc; rep from * to beg ch-3; join in 2nd ch of beg ch-3.

Rnd 2:
Sl st in next ch-1 sp, 2 sc in same sp and in each rem ch-1 sp; join in first sc.

Finish off and weave in all ends.

Layout

Start border here

Lollipop Confection
designed by Linda Mershon

This pleasing new design is created with two motifs. The larger motifs with spiral centers are joined as you make the loopy outer round. The smaller filler motifs are added later.

Lollipop Confection

Size:
About 47" x 60"

Materials:
Worsted weight yarn, 25 oz (1750 yds, 750 gms) variegated; 26 oz (1820 yds, 780 gms) lt purple

Note: *Our photographed afghan was made with Red Heart® Super Saver®, Gumdrop #952 and Lilac #353.*

Size I (5.5mm) crochet hook, or size required for gauge
Size 16 tapestry needle

Gauge:
7 sc = 2"

Instructions

Large Motifs

Note: *Refer to Layout A for placement of motifs.*

Motif A:
With variegated, ch 2.

Note: *Rnds 1 through 6 are worked in continuous rnds; do not join. Mark beg of each rnd. To change color, work last st until 2 lps remain on hook. With new color, YO and draw through 2 lps on hook. Cut old color.*

Rnd 1 (right side):
6 sc in 2nd ch from hook.

Rnd 2:
2 sc in each sc—12 sc.

Rnd 3:
(Sc in next sc, 2 sc in next sc) 6 times—18 sc.

Rnd 4:
(Sc in next 2 sc, 2 sc in next sc) 6 times—24 sc.

Rnd 5:
(Sc in next 3 sc, 2 sc in next sc) 6 times—30 sc.

Rnd 6:
(Sc in next 4 sc, 2 sc in next sc) 5 times; sc in next 4 sc, 2 sc in next sc; changing to lt purple in last sc—36 sc.

Note: *Remaining rnds are joined.*

Rnd 7:
(Sc in next 3 sc, ch 5) 12 times; join in first sc.

Rnd 8:
* Sl st in next sc, 7 hdc in next ch-5 sp—petal made, sk next sc; rep from * 10 times more; sl st in next sc, 7 hdc in next ch-5 sp—petal made; sk joining sl st; join in next sl st—12 petals. Finish off.

Motif B:
Work same as Motif A through Rnd 7.

Rnd 8 (joining rnd):
(Sl st in next sc, petal in next ch-5 sp, sk next sc) 10 times; sl st in next sc, 4 hdc in next ch-5 sp; hold wrong side of last completed motif facing wrong side of working motif; on completed motif, sl st in 4th hdc of any petal; on working motif, 3 hdc in same ch-5 sp—joined petal made; sk next sc, sl st in next sc, 4 hdc in next ch-5 sp; on completed motif, sl st in 4th hdc of next petal; on working motif, 3 hdc in same ch-5 sp—joined petal made; sk joining sl st; join in next sl st. Finish off.

Motif C:
Work same as Motif A through Rnd 7.

Rnd 8 (joining rnd):
(Sl st in next sc, petal in next ch-5 sp, sk next sc) 10 times; sl st in next sc, 4 hdc in next ch-5 sp; hold wrong side of last completed motif facing wrong side of working motif; on completed motif, sk next 4 petals from first joining; sl st in 4th hdc of next petal; on working motif, 3 hdc in

Layout A

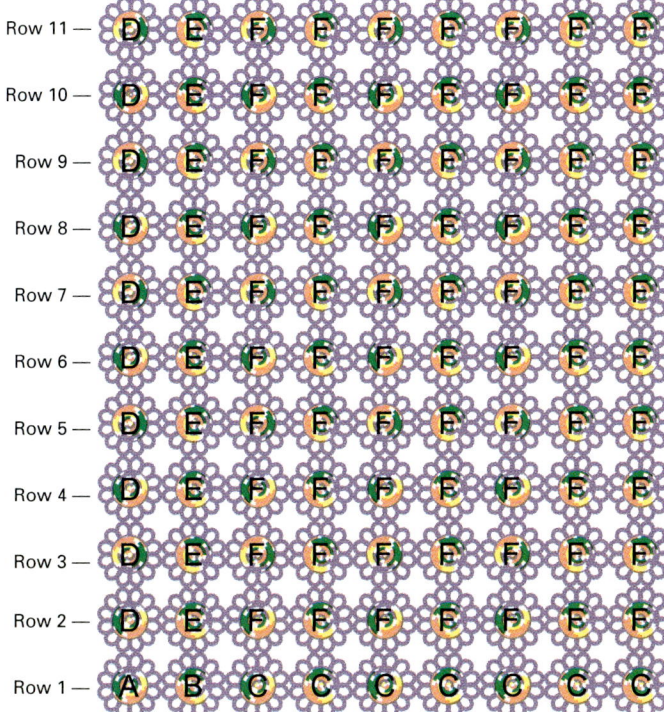

same ch-5 sp—joined petal made; sk next sc, sl st in next sc, 4 hdc in next ch-5 sp; on completed motif, sl st in 4th hdc of next petal; on working motif, 3 hdc in same ch-5 sp—joined petal made; sk joining sl st; join in next sl st. Finish off.

Motif D:
Work same as Motif A through Rnd 7.

Rnd 8 (joining rnd):
(Sl st in next sc, petal in next ch-5 sp, sk next sc) 10 times; sl st in next sc, 4 hdc in next ch-5 sp; holding wrong side of Motif A facing wrong side of working motif; on Motif A, sk next 7 petals from last joined petal, sl st in 4th hdc of next petal; on working motif, 3 hdc in same ch-5 sp—joined petal made; sk next sc, sl st in next sc, 4 hdc in next ch-5 sp; on Motif A, sl st in 4th hdc of next petal; on working motif, 3 hdc in same ch-5 sp—joined petal made; sk joining sl st; join in next sl st. Finish off.

Motif E:
Work same as Motif A through Rnd 7.

Rnd 8 (joining rnd):
(Sl st in next sc, petal in next ch-5 sp, sk next sc) 7 times; sl st in next sc, 4 hdc in next ch-5 sp; holding wrong side of last completed motif facing wrong side of working motif; on completed motif, sk next 7 petals from first joined petal, sl st in 4th hdc of next petal; on working motif, 3 hdc in same ch-5 sp—joined petal made; sk next sc, sl st in next sc, 4 hdc in next ch-5 sp; on completed motif, sl st in 4th hdc of next petal; on working motif, 3 hdc in same ch-5 sp—joined petal made; sk next sc, sl st in next sc, petal in next ch-5 sp; sk next sc, sl st in next sc, 4 hdc in next ch-5 sp; hold wrong side of Motif B facing wrong side of working motif; on Motif B, sk next petal from joined petal, sl st in 4th hdc of next petal; on working motif, 3 hdc in same ch-5 sp; sk next sc, sl st in next sc, 4 hdc in next ch-5 sp; on Motif B, sl st in 4th hdc of next petal; on working motif, 3 hdc in same ch-5 sp; sk joining sl st; join in next sl st. Finish off.

Motif F:
Work same as Motif A through Rnd 7.

Row 8 (joining rnd):
(Sl st in next sc, petal in next ch-5 sp, sk next sc) 7 times; sl st in next sc, 4 hdc in next ch-5 sp; holding wrong side of last completed motif facing wrong side of working motif; on completed motif, sk next 4 petals from first joined petal, sl st in 4th hdc of next petal; on working motif, 3 hdc in same ch-5 sp—joined petal made; sk next sc, sl st in next sc, 4 hdc in next ch-5 sp; on completed motif, sl st in 4th hdc of next petal; on working motif, 3 hdc in same ch-5 sp—joined petal made; sk next sc, sl st in next sc, petal in next ch-5 sp; sk next sc, sl st in next sc, 4 hdc in next ch-5 sp; hold wrong side of Motif C facing wrong side of working motif; on Motif C, sk next petal from joined petal, sl st in 4th hdc of next petal; on working motif, 3 hdc in same ch-5 sp; sk next sc, sl st in next sc, 4 hdc in next ch-5 sp; on Motif C, sl st in 4th hdc of next petal; on working motif, 3 hdc in same ch-5 sp; sk joining sl st; join in next sl st. Finish off.

Referring to **Layout A**, work remaining D, E, and F Motifs in same manner, joining to motifs on prev rows.

continued

Lollipop Confection

Filler Motif (make 80)

Note: Filler motifs are worked between each group of four joined motifs (see **Diagram A**). There are 4 unused petals, one on each motif. Filler motis will be joined in 4th hdc of each of these petals and in joining sl sts.

Diagram A

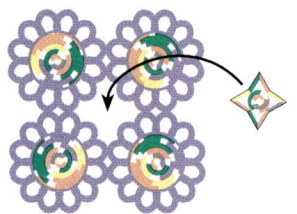

With variegated, ch 2.

Rnd 1:
6 sc in 2nd ch from hook. Do not join.

Rnd 2:
2 sc in each sc—12 sc. Do not join.

Rnd 3:
(Sc in next 3 sc, ch 5) 4 times; join in first sc.

Rnd 4 (joining rnd):
Sl st in next sc; working in sp between Motifs A, B, D and E, hold wrong side of any completed motif facing wrong side of working motif; ∗ † on completed motif, sl st in 4th hdc of unused petal; on working motif, 4 hdc in next ch-5 sp; sl st in next joining of completed motifs, 3 hdc in same ch-5 sp †; sk next sc, sl st in next sc; rep from ∗ twice more, then rep from † to † once; sk joining sl st; join in next sl st. Finish off.

Work remaining filler motifs in center of each group of four joined motifs, **Layout B**.

Weave in all ends.

Layout B

Old Cathedral *designed by Linda Mershon*

Use your little bits of waiting, visiting and watching TV time for making a triangle for this afghan and you'll soon have enough triangles to join into one of the most beautiful afghans ever!

Old Cathedral

Size:
About 49" x 49"

Materials:
Worsted weight yarn, 28½ oz (1995 yds, 855 gms) rose; 32 oz (2240 yds, 960 gms) off white

Note: Our photographed afghan was made with Bernat® Pounder, Natural #3008 and Med Rose #3005.

Size H (5mm) crochet hook, or size required for gauge
Size 16 tapestry needle

Gauge:
7 sc = 2"

Pattern Stitches

Double Triple Crochet (dtrc):
YO 3 times, draw up lp in st indicated, (YO, draw through 2 lps on hook) 4 times—dtrc made.

Cluster (CL):
Keeping last lp of each dc on hook, dc in each of next 6 sts, YO and draw through all 7 lps on hook—CL made.

Instructions

Motifs

Motif A (make 56):
With rose, ch 5; join to form a ring.

Rnd 1 (right side):
Ch 3, 2 dc in ring; ch 5, (3 dc in ring, ch 5) twice; join in 3rd ch of beg ch-3—three 3-dc groups.

Rnd 2:
Sl st in next 2 dc and in next ch-5 sp, ch 3 (counts as a dc), in same sp work (2 dc, ch 5, 3 dc); * ch 2, in next ch-5 sp work (3 dc, ch 5, 3 dc); rep from * once more; ch 2; join in 3rd ch of beg ch-3. Finish off.

Rnd 3:
With off white make slip knot on hook and join with an sc in first ch of any ch-5 sp; sc in next ch; * in next ch work (sc, ch 3, sc); sc in next 2 chs, in next 3 dc, and in next 2 chs; sc in next 3 dc, sc in next 2 chs of next ch-5 sp; rep from * once more; in next ch work (sc, ch 3, sc); sc in next 2 chs, in next 3 dc, in next 2 chs, and in next 3 dc; join in joining sc.

Rnd 4:
Ch 1, sc in same sc, in next 2 sc, and in first ch of next ch-3 sp; in next ch work (sc, ch 3, sc); * sc in next ch, in next 14 sc, and in first ch of next ch-3 sp; in next ch work (sc, ch 3, sc); rep from * once more; sc in next ch and in next 11 sc; join in first sc.

Rnd 5:
Ch 1, sc in same sc, in next 4 sc, and in first ch of next ch-3 sp; in next ch work (sc, ch 3, sc); sc in next ch, in next 18 sc, and in first ch of next ch-3 sp; in next ch work (sc, ch 3, sc); rep from * once more; sc in next ch and in next 13 sc; join in first sc. Finish off.

Rnd 6:
With rose make slip knot on hook and join with an sc in first ch of any ch-3 sp; in next ch work (sc, ch 3, sc); *† sc in next 7 sts, working over Rnds 3, 4, and 5, dtrc (see Pattern Stitches) in unused lp of 3rd ch of ch-5 sp on Rnd 2; sk next 3 dc on same rnd, dtrc in unused lp of first ch of next ch-2 sp on same rnd; on working rnd, sk next 2 sc, sc in next 6 sc; on Rnd 2, dtrc in unused lp of next ch, sk next 3 dc and next 2 chs of next ch-5 sp, dtrc in unused lp of next ch †; on working rnd, sc in next 6 sc and in next ch; in next ch work (sc, ch 3, sc); rep from * once more, then rep from † to † once; on working rnd, sc in next 6 sc; join in joining sc. Finish off.

Motif B (make 48):
With off white, ch 2.

Rnds 1 through 6:
Rep Rnds 1 through 6 of Motif A, using off white for Rnds 1 and 2, rose for Rnds 3 through 5, and off white for Rnd 6.

Assembly

Referring to **Layout** for placement, join motifs in rows. To join motifs, hold 2 motifs with right sides together and carefully matching stitches, with matching color, sl st in BLs only along one side, beginning and ending with 2nd ch of corners. Join remaining motifs in same manner.

Edging

Hold afghan with right side facing you and one straight end at top; join rose in 2nd ch of ch-3 sp in upper right-hand corner.

Rnd 1 (right side):
Ch 3 (counts as a dc), 2 dc in same ch—corner made; dc in next ch, † dc in next 26 sts, dc in next 2 chs, in next joining and in next 2 chs †; rep from † to † 5 times more; dc in next 26 sts, dc in next ch, 3 dc in next ch—corner made; working along next side, dc in next ch; †† dc in next 25 sts, CL (see Pattern Stitches on page 80) over next st, next 4 chs, and next st; dc in next 25 sts, dc in next 2 chs, in next joining, and in next 2 chs ††; rep from †† to †† twice more; dc in next 25 sts, CL over next st, next 4 chs, and next st; dc in next 25 sts, dc in next ch, 3 dc in next ch—corner made; working along next side, dc in next ch; rep from † to † 6 times; dc in next 26 sts, dc in next ch, 3 dc in next ch—corner made; dc in next ch; rep from †† to †† 3 times; dc in next 25 sts, CL over next st, next 4 chs, and next st; dc in next 25 sts and in next ch; join in 3rd ch of beg ch-3. Finish off.

Rnd 2:
With off white make slip knot on hook and join with an sc in 2nd dc of any corner, 2 sc in 2nd dc—corner made; * sc in each st to 2nd dc of next corner; 3 sc in 2nd dc—corner made; rep from * twice more; sc in each st to joining sc; join in joining sc.

Finish off and weave in all ends.

Layout

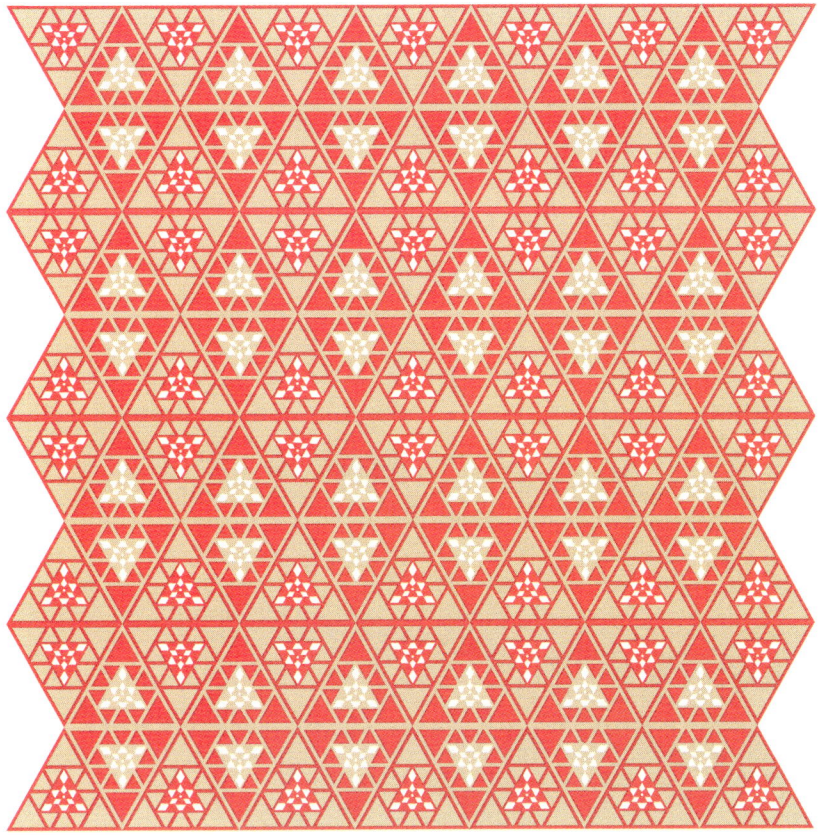

Simply Scrumptious
designed by Denise Black

Designed using the double-ended crochet hook, this afghan is reversible! Perfect in off-white and a soft color, you'll love wrapping yourself in this afghan.

Size:
About 45" x 60" before fringe

Materials:
Worsted weight yarn, 38 oz (2660 yds, 1140 gms) off white; 35 oz (2450 yds, 1050 gms) peach

Note: *Our photograped afghan was made with Caron® Sayelle®, Fisherman #336 and Canyon Coral #2051.*

Size K (6.50mm) double-ended crochet hook, or size required for gauge
Size 16 tapestry needle

Gauge:
4 sc = 1"

Instructions
With off white, ch 180.

Row 1:
Working through BLs only, insert hook in 2nd ch from hook, YO and draw through forming a lp on hook; * insert hook in next ch, YO and draw through; rep from * across—180 lps on hook. Slide all lps to opposite end of hook and turn work. Do not cut off white.

Row 2:
To work lps off hook, with peach make slip knot on hook; working from left to right, draw slip knot through first lp on hook; * YO, draw through 2 lps on hook (one of each color); rep from * until one lp remains on hook. Do not turn work.

Row 3:
Continuing with peach and working right to left, sk first vertical bar; * insert hook under next vertical bar and draw up lp; rep from * across—180 lps on hook. Slide work to opposite end of hook and turn work. Do not cut peach.

Row 4:
With off white, YO and draw through one lp on hook; * YO and draw through 2 lps on hook (one of each color); rep from * across until one lp remains on hook. Do not turn work.

Row 5:
Sk first vertical bar, insert hook under next vertical bar, YO and draw through; * ch 1, YO, sk next vertical bar, insert hook under next vertical bar, YO, and draw through; rep from * across. Slide work to opposite end of hook and turn work.

continued

Simply Scrumptious

Row 6:
With peach, YO and draw through one lp on hook; * YO and draw through 2 lps on hook (one of each color); rep from * across until one lp remains on hook. Do not turn work.

Row 7:
Continuing with peach and working right to left, sk first vertical bar; * insert hook under next vertical bar and draw up lp; rep from * across—180 lps on hook. Slide work to opposite end of hook and turn work. Do not cut peach.

Rows 8 and 9:
Rep Rows 6 and 7 with off white.

Rows 10 and 11:
Rep Rows 6 and 7.

Rep Rows 4 through 11 until piece measures about 58", ending with a Row 8.

Next Row:
Sk first vertical bar; * insert hook under next vertical bar, YO and draw through both lps on hook; rep from * across.

Finish off and weave in all ends.

Fringe
Following Fringe instructions on page 159, make Single Knot Fringe. Cut 30" strands of each color; use 4 strands of each color for each knot. Working across each short end of afghan, tie knots evenly spaced (about every 3rd st). Trim ends even.

City Sophistication

If you think an afghan can't be chic and modern, we've got a few surprises for you. These are afghan designs that let you show your style!

Autumn Afternoon	86
City Escape	89
Impressionist Ripple	91
Night and Day	94
Ombré for Your Hombré	97
Pavé Diamonds	99
Sonata	102
Spanish Tiles	107
Twilight Tapestry	110

Autumn Afternoon
designed by Eleanor Albano-Miles

Using the most up-to-date home decor colorations this afghan is a fashionable home accessory. This interesting pattern is created by adding the chevron design to quick-to-make crocheted squares.

Size:
About 55" x 73½"

Materials:
Worsted weight yarn, 47 oz (3290 yds, 1410 gms) green; 8 oz (560 yds, 240 gms) each, olive green, rust, and rose

Note: *Our photographed afghan was made with Lion Brand® Wool Ease®, Seaspray #123, Loden #177, Terracotta #134, and Guava #133.*

Size I (5.5mm) crochet hook, or size required for gauge
Size 16 tapestry needle

Gauge:
4 dc = 1"

Instructions

Motif (make 48)
With green, ch 33.

Row 1 (right side):
Dc in 4th ch from hook (3 skipped chs count as a dc) and in each rem ch—31 dc. Ch 3 (counts as first dc on following rows), turn.

Row 2:
Dc in each dc and in 3rd ch of beg 3 skipped chs. Ch 3, turn.

Row 3:
Dc in next 3 dc, (ch 1, sk next dc, dc in next dc) 12 times; dc in next 2 dc and in 3rd ch of turning ch-3. Ch 3, turn.

Row 4:
Dc in next 3 dc, (ch 1, dc in next dc) 12 times; dc in next 2 dc and in 3rd ch of turning ch-3. Ch 3, turn.

Rows 5 through 14:
Rep Row 4.

Row 15:
Dc in each ch-1 sp, in each dc, and in 3rd ch of turning ch-3. Ch 3, turn.

Row 16:
Dc in each dc and in 3rd ch of turning ch-3. Ch 1, turn.

continued

Autumn Afternoon

Edging:
In first dc work (sc, ch 2, sc)—corner made; * sc in each dc to turning ch; in 3rd ch of turning ch-3 work (sc, ch 2, sc)—corner made; working along next side in sps formed by edge dc and turning chs, 2 sc in each sp; working along next side in unused lps of beg ch, in next lp work (sc, ch 2, sc)—corner made; sc in next 29 lps, in next lp work (sc, ch 2, sc)—corner made; working along next side in sps formed by edge dc and turning chs, 2 sc in each sp; join in first sc. Finish off.

Top Stitching:
Note: Top stitching is worked vertically in ch-1 sps of Rows 3 through 14, and horizontally over posts (see Stitch Guide on page 160) of sts. Refer to **Diagram A** for placement of following rows.

Diagram A

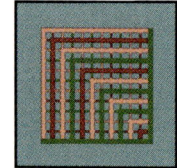

Horizontal Row 1:
Hold motif with right side facing you and Row 16 at top; join olive green around post of 5th dc on Row 3; ch 1, sc around post of same dc; * ch 1, sc around post of next dc; rep from * 9 times more. Finish off.

Vertical Row 1:
Hold motif with right side facing you and Row 16 at top; join olive green in first ch-1 sp on Row 3, ch 1, sc in same sp; (ch 1, sc in first ch-1 sp on row above) 10 times. Finish off.

Horizontal Row 2:
Join rust around post of 5th dc on next row above last worked horizontal row, ch 1, sc around post of same dc; * ch 1, sc around post of next dc; rep from * 9 times more. Finish off.

Vertical Row 2:
Join rust in next ch-1 sp on Row 3 to left of last worked vertical row, ch 1, sc in same sp; (ch 1, sc in next ch-1 sp on row above) 10 times. Finish off.

Continue working in same manner, joining horizontal rows around post of 5th dc on next row above, and vertical rows in ch-1 sps to left of prev vertical row, alternating rose, olive green, and rust, and ending with rose.

Draw all ends to wrong side and weave in.

Note: Before joining squares always check placement of top stitching.

Assembly

Referring to **Diagram B** for placement, join 4 motifs. To join motifs, hold 2 motifs with right sides together and carefully matching stitches; with tapestry needle and green, sew together with overcast stitch (see Stitch Guide on page 160) through BLs only along one side. Join remaining 2 motifs to form square. Join remaining motifs in same manner to form 11 additional squares. Referring to **Layout** for placement of squares, join squares in same manner, being sure all four-corner junctions are firmly joined.

Diagram B

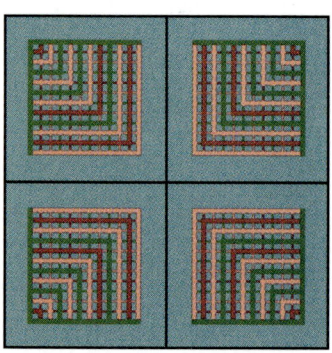

Layout

Edging

Hold afghan with right side facing you and one short end at top; with green make slip knot on hook and join with an sc in ch-2 sp in upper right-hand corner; ch 1, sc in same corner; working in BLs only, * sc in each sc and in each joining to next corner ch-2 sp; in corner ch-2 sp work (sc, ch 1, sc); rep from * 3 times more; sc in each sc and each joining to first sc; join in first sc.

Finish off and weave in ends.

City Escape designed by Mary Lamb Becker

In two tones of neutral grey, this striking design is a wonderful room accent. The darker grey background is crocheted first and then the lighter grey trim rows are added.

City Escape

Size:
About 44" x 62" before fringe

Materials:
Worsted weight yarn, 48 oz (3360 yds, 1440 gms) dk grey; 11½ oz (805 yds, 345 gms) lt grey

Note: Our photographed afghan was made with Red Heart® Super Saver, Grey Heather #400 and Light Grey #341.

Size I (5.5mm) crochet hook, or size required for gauge
Size 16 tapestry needle

Gauge:
3 dc = 1"

Pattern Stitch

Front Post Single Crochet (FPsc):
Insert hook from front to back to front around post (see Stitch Guide on page 160) of st indicated, draw up lp, YO and draw through both lps on hook—FPsc made.

Instructions

With dk grey, ch 163.

Row 1 (right side):
Sc in 2nd ch from hook and in next 6 chs; * (sc in next ch, ch 1, sk next ch, sc in next ch) 8 times; sc in next 7 chs; rep from * 4 times more. Ch 3 (counts as first dc on following rows), turn.

Row 2:
Dc in next 6 sc; * in each of next 8 ch-1 sps work (dc, ch 1, dc); sk next sc, dc in next 7 sc; rep from * 4 times more. Ch 1, turn.

Row 3:
Sc in first 7 dc; * † in each of next 8 ch-1 sps work (sc, ch 1, sc); sk next dc †; sc in next 7 dc; rep from * 3 times more, then rep from † to † once; sc in next 6 dc and in 3rd ch of turning ch-3. Ch 3, turn.

Rows 4 through 133:
Rep Rows 2 and 3, 65 times more. At end of last row, do not ch 3.

Finish off and weave in all ends.

Trim Rows
Hold afghan with right side facing you and last row worked at top. On first 7-dc section from right, mark 6th dc from right on Rows 2, 6, 10, and every 4th row to top of afghan. Mark 2nd dc from right on Rows 4, 8, 12, and every 4th row to top of afghan. With lt grey make slip knot on hook and join with an FPsc (see Pattern Stitch) around marked dc on Row 2; 2 FPsc around same dc; * ch 3, 3 FPsc around next marked dc 2 rows above; rep from * to top of afghan. Finish off.

Repeat on five remaining 7-dc sections.

Fringe
Following Fringe instructions on page 159, make Single Knot Fringe. Cut 30" strands of each color; use 4 strands of each color for each knot. Working across each short end of afghan, tie knots evenly spaced (about every 3rd st). Trim ends even.

Impressionist Ripple
designed by Kathy Wesley

The brushed bulky yarn we used for this afghan makes it a quick and cozy choice. Choosing two solid colors that don't match the variegated shades too closely will result in a more stunning look.

Impressionist Ripple

Size:
About 48" x 66"

Materials:
Brushed bulky weight yarn, 13½ oz (945 yds, 405 gms) blue; 15 oz (1050 yds, 450 gms) off white; 28 oz (1960 yds, 840 gms) variegated

Note: *Our photographed afghan was made with Lion Brand® Jiffy®, Heather Blue #111, Fisherman #099 and Salem #330.*

Size I (5.5mm) crochet hook, or size required for gauge
Size 16 tapestry needle

Gauge:
10 dc = 3"

Pattern Stitch

Cluster (CL):
Keeping last lp of each dc on hook, 3 dc in st indicated; YO and draw through all 4 lps on hook—CL made.

Instructions

Note: *To change colors, work until 2 lps of last st remain on hook. With new color, YO and draw through 2 lps on hook. Cut old color.*

With blue, ch 188.

Row 1 (right side):
Sc in 2nd ch from hook and in each rem ch, changing to variegated in last sc—187 sc. Cut blue. Ch 2 (counts as first dc on following rows), turn.

Row 2:
Sk first 3 sc, working in FLs only, (3 dc in next sc, sk next 2 sc) twice; in next sc work (3 dc, ch 3, 3 dc); * † sk next 2 sc, (3 dc in next sc, sk next 2 sc) twice † ; CL (see Pattern Stitch) in next sc; sk next 2 sc, CL in next sc; sk next 2 sc, (3 dc in next sc, sk next 2 sc) twice; in next sc work (3 dc, ch 3, 3 dc); rep from * 7 times more, then rep from † to † once; dc in next sc. Ch 2, turn.

> **Note:** *When instructed to work in sps, work in sps between 3-dc groups or CLs.*

Row 3:
Sk first sp (between turning ch and next 3-dc group), 3 dc in each of next 2 sps; in next ch-3 sp work (3 dc, ch 3, 3 dc); * 3 dc in each of next 2 sps; CL in next sp; sk sp between CLs, CL in next sp; 3 dc in each of next 2 sps; in next ch-3 sp work (3 dc, ch 3, 3 dc); rep from * 7 times more; 3 dc in each of next 2 sps; dc in next sp (between last 3-dc group and turning ch). Ch 2, turn.

Row 4:
Sk first sp (between turning ch and next 3-dc group), 3 dc in each of next 2 sps; in next ch-3 sp work (3 dc, ch 3, 3 dc); * 3 dc in each of next 2 sps; CL in next sp; sk sp between CLs, CL in next sp; 3 dc in each of next 2 sps; in next ch-3 sp work (3 dc, ch 3, 3 dc); rep from * 7 times more; 3 dc in each of next 2 sps; dc in next sp (between last 3-dc group and turning ch), changing to blue; cut variegated. Ch 1, turn.

Row 5:
Sc in first dc, sk next dc, sc in next 8 dc; * 3 sc in next ch-3 sp; sc in next 9 dc, sk next 2 CLs, sc in next 9 dc; rep from * 7 times more; 3 sc in next ch-3 sp; sc in next 8 dc, sk next dc, sc in 2nd ch of turning ch-2, changing to off white. Ch 2, turn.

Row 6:
Sk first 2 sc, working in FLs only, dc in next 8 sc; * 3 dc in next sc; dc in next 9 sc, sk next 2 sc, dc in next 9 sc; rep from * 7 times more; 3 dc in next sc; dc in next 8 sc, sk next sc, dc in next sc, changing to blue; cut off white. Ch 1, turn.

Row 7:
Sc in first dc, sk next 2 dc, sc in next 7 dc; * 3 sc in next dc; sc in next 9 dc, sk next 2 dc, sc in next 9 dc; rep from * 7 times more; 3 sc in next dc; sc in next 7 dc, sk next 2 dc, sc in 2nd ch of turning ch-2, changing to off white; cut blue. Ch 2, turn.

Row 8:
Sk first sc, working in FLs only, dc in next 8 sc; * 3 dc in next sc; dc in next 9 sc, sk next 2 sc, dc in next 9 sc; rep from * 7 times more; 3 dc in next sc; dc in next 9 sc changing to blue in last sc; cut off white. Ch 1, turn.

Row 9:
Sc in first dc, sk next 2 dc, sc in next 7 dc; * 3 sc in next dc; sc in next 9 dc, sk next 2 dc, sc in next 9 dc; rep from * 7 times more; 3 sc in next dc; sc in next 7 dc, sk next 2 dc, sc in 2nd ch of turning ch-2, changing to variegated; cut blue. Ch 2, turn.

Rep Rows 2 through 9 until piece measures about 66", ending with a Row 5. At end of last row, do not ch 2.

Finish off and weave in all ends.

Night and Day
designed by Linda Mershon

Black and white yarn and a nifty little square combine to make this a decidedly different afghan. The positive/negative effect is dramatic in black and white, but could be equally impressive in other color shades.

Size:
About 51" x 61"

Materials:
Worsted weight yarn, 39 oz (2730 yds, 1170 gms) black; 34½ oz (2415 yds, 1035 gms) white

Note: *Our photographed afghan was made with Caron® One Pound, Black #0503 and Bright White #0501.*

Size H (5mm) crochet hook, or size required for gauge
Size 16 tapestry needle

Gauge:
7 sc = 2"

Pattern Stitch

Front Post Double Triple Crochet (FPdtrc):
YO 3 times, insert hook from front to back to front around post (see Stitch Guide on page 160) of st indicated, draw up lp, **(**YO, draw through 2 lps on hook**)** 4 times—FPdtrc made.

Instructions

Motif A (make 180)
With black, ch 6; join to form a ring.

Rnd 1 (right side):
Ch 1, 12 sc in ring; join in first sc. Change to white by drawing lp through; cut black.

Rnd 2:
Ch 1, 2 sc in same sc and in each rem sc; join in first sc—24 sc.

Rnd 3:
Ch 3 **(**counts as a dc**)**, dc in next 5 sc, ch 3, **(**dc in next 6 dc, ch 3**)** 3 times; join in 3rd ch of beg ch-3. Change to black; cut white.

Rnd 4:
Ch 1, sc in same ch as joining and in next dc; * † FPdtrc **(**see Pattern Stitch**)** around post of next sc on 2nd rnd below; FPdtrc around post of next sc on 2nd rnd below; on working rnd, sk next 2 dc, sc in next 2 dc and in next ch, in next ch work **(**sc, ch 3, sc**)** †; sc in next ch and next 2 dc, sk next 4 sc on Rnd 2; rep from * twice more, then rep from † to † once; join in first sc. Finish off, leaving an 8" end for sewing.

continued

Night and Day

Motif B (make 90)
Work same as Motif A, reversing colors.

Assembly

Referring to **Layout A** for placement, join six A Motifs and three B Motifs to form a square. To join motifs, hold two motifs with right sides together and carefully matching stitches; with tapestry needle and long end, sew with overcast stitch (see Stitch Guide on page 160) through BLs only along one side edge. Sew additional motifs together is same manner to form square.

Layout A

Rep with remaining motifs to form 29 additional squares.

Referring to **Layout B**, sew squares together in same manner, having all squares in same position.

Edging

Hold afghan with right side facing you and one short end at top; with black make slip knot on hook and join with an sc in ch-3 sp in upper right-hand corner.

Rnd 1 (right side):
2 sc in same sp—beg corner made; sc in next 10 sts; † sc in next ch-3 sp, in next joining, in next ch-3 sp, and in next 10 sts †; rep from † to † 13 times more; 3 sc in next corner ch-3 sp—corner made; sc in next 10 sts; rep from † to † 17 times; 3 sc in next corner ch-3 sp—corner made; sc in next 10 sts; rep from † to † 14 times; 3 sc in next corner ch-3 sp—corner made; sc in next 10 sts; rep from † to † 17 times; join in joining sc. Change to white by drawing lp through; cut black.

Rnd 2:
Ch 1, sc in same sc, in next sc work corner; * sc in each sc to 2nd sc of next corner; in 2nd sc work corner ; rep from * twice more; sc in each sc to first sc; join in first sc.

Finish off and weave in all ends.

Layout B

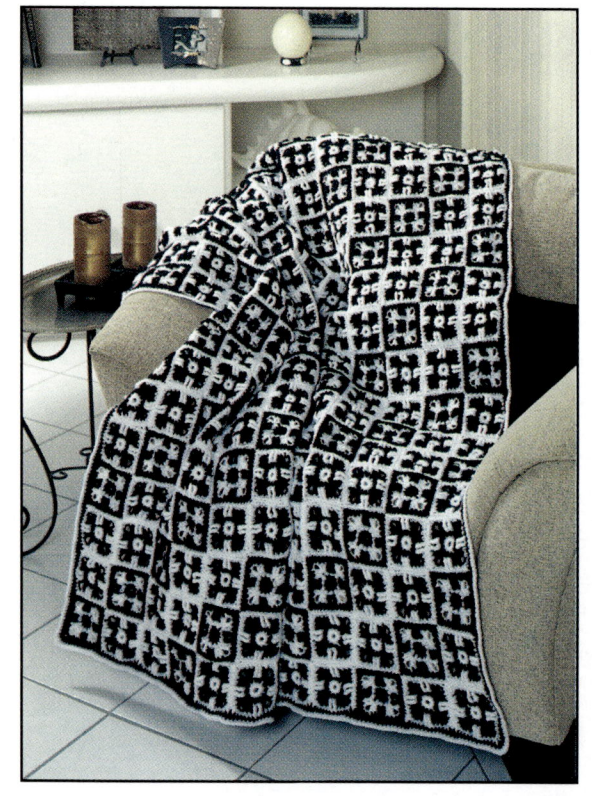

Ombré for Your Hombré
designed by Kathy Wesley

*S*oft, bulky yarn in variegated skeins makes this a no-fuss afghan for beginners or those who really want to relax as they crochet. The beautiful stripings are a result of the ombré yarn.

Ombré for Your Ombré

Size:
About 45" x 66"

Materials:
Bulky weight yarn, 59 oz (2065 yds, 1770 gms) ombré
   Note: Our photographed afghan was made with Lion Brand® Homespun®, Prairie #335.
Size I (5.5mm) crochet hook, or size required for gauge
Size 16 tapestry needle

Gauge:
4 pattern reps = 5"
one pattern rep = (sc, ch 3, 3 dc)

Instructions

Ch 170.

Row 1 (right side):
Sc in 2nd ch from hook and in each rem ch—169 sc. Ch 1, turn.

Row 2:
Sc in first sc; * ch 3, sk next 3 sc, sc in next sc; rep from * 41 times more. Ch 3, turn.

Row 3:
3 dc in first sc; in each sc to last sc work (sc, ch 3, 3 dc); sc in last sc. Ch 6 (counts as first dc and ch-3 sp on following rows), turn.

Row 4:
Sk next 3 dc, sc in next ch-3 sp; * ch 3, sk next 3 dc, sc in next ch-3 sp; rep from * across. Ch 1, turn.

Row 5:
Sc in first sc; in each sc to turning ch-6 work (3 dc, ch 3, sc); sk next 3 chs of turning ch, 4 dc in next ch. Ch 1, turn.

Row 6:
Sc in first dc; * ch 3, sc in next ch-3 sp; rep from * to last sc; ch 3, dc in last sc. Ch 3, turn.

Row 7:
3 dc in first dc; in each sc to last sc work (sc, ch 3, 3 dc); sc in last sc. Ch 6 (counts as a dc and a ch-3 sp), turn.

Rep Rows 4 through 7 until piece measures about 62".

Rep Rows 4 through 6 once. At end of last row, do not ch 3. Ch 1, turn.

Last Row:
Sc in first sc; * 3 sc in next ch-3 sp; sc in next sc; rep from * across.

Finish off and weave in all ends.

Pavé Diamonds *designed by Becky Stevens*

For classic good looks and an afghan that will look great in any setting there's nothing like a Fisherman. Finished with elegant triple knot fringe, the advanced crocheter will enjoy making and giving this afghan.

Pavé Diamonds

Size:
About 48" x 60" before fringe

Materials:
Worsted weight yarn, 77 oz (5390 yds, 2310 gms) off white

Note: *Our photographed afghan was made with Red Heart® Classic™, Off White #3.*

Size K (6.5mm) crochet hook, or size required for gauge
Size 16 tapestry needle

Gauge:
3 sts = 1"

Pattern Stitches

Cable Twist (CT):
YO, insert hook from front to back to front around post (see Stitch Guide on page 160) of next st on 2nd row below; YO and draw through 2 lps on hook, YO, insert hook from front to back to front of same st, YO and draw through 2 lps on hook, YO and draw through all 3 lps on hook—CT made.

Split Cable Twist (split CT):
[YO, insert hook from front to back to front around post (see Stitch Guide on page 160) of next CT, YO and draw through 2 lps on hook] twice; YO and draw through all 3 lps on hook—split CT made.

Pebble Stitch (pebble st):
Draw up lp in st indicated, ch 3, keeping ch-3 to front of work, YO and draw through 2 lps on hook—pebble st made.

Instructions
Ch 162.

Row 1 (right side):
Sc in 2nd ch from hook and in each rem ch—161 sc. Ch 1, turn.

Row 2:
Sc in each sc. Ch 1, turn.

> **Note:** *On working row, always skip st behind CT.*

Row 3:
Sc in first 2 sc; * CT (see Pattern Stitches) around next sc on 2nd row below; on working row, sc in next sc, pebble st (see Pattern Stitches) in next sc; (sc in next sc, pebble st in next sc) 4 times; sc in next sc; rep from * 12 times more; CT around next sc on 2nd row below; on working row, sc in next 2 sc. Ch 1, turn.

Row 4:
Sc in each st. Ch 1, turn.

Row 5:
Sc in first sc, pebble st in next sc; sc in next sc, CT around next CT on 2nd row below; * † on working row, (sc in next sc, pebble st in next sc) 4 times; sc in next sc †; CT around next CT on 2nd row below; on working row, sc in next sc, CT around same CT on 2nd row below as last CT made; rep from * 11 times more, then rep from † to † once; CT around next CT on 2nd row below; on working row, sc in next sc, pebble st in next sc; sc in next sc. Ch 1, turn.

Row 6:
Rep Row 4.

Row 7:
Sc in first 2 sc, pebble st in next sc; sc in next sc; * † CT around next CT on 2nd row below; on working row, (sc in next sc, pebble st in next sc) 3 times; sc in next sc †; CT around next CT on 2nd row below; on working row, sc in next sc, pebble st in next sc; sc in next sc; rep from * 11 times more, then rep from † to † once; CT around next CT on 2nd row below; on working row, sc in next sc, pebble st in next sc; sc in next sc. Ch 1, turn.

Row 8:
Rep Row 4.

Row 9:
Sc in first sc, (pebble st in next sc, sc in next sc) twice; * CT around next CT on 2nd row below; on working row, (sc in next sc, pebble st in next sc) twice; sc in next sc; rep from * 25 times more. Ch 1, turn.

Row 10:
Rep Row 4.

Row 11:
Sc in first 2 sc, (pebble st in next sc, sc in next sc) twice; * CT around next CT on 2nd row below; on working row, sc in next sc, pebble st in next sc; sc in next sc, CT around next CT on 2nd row below; on working row, (sc in next sc, pebble st in next sc) 3 times; sc in next sc; rep from * 11 times more; CT around next CT on 2nd row below; on working row, sc in next sc, pebble st in next sc; sc in next sc, CT around next CT on 2nd row below; on working row, (sc in next sc, pebble st in next sc) twice; sc in next 2 sc. Ch 1, turn.

Row 12:
Rep Row 4.

Row 13:
Sc in first sc, pebble st in next sc; (sc in next sc, pebble st in next sc) twice; sc in next sc; *† CT around next CT on 2nd row below; on working row, sc in next sc, CT around next CT on 2nd row below †; on working row, (sc in next sc, pebble st in next sc) 4 times; sc in next sc; rep from * 11 times more, then rep from † to † once; on working row, (sc in next sc, pebble st in next sc) 3 times; sc in next sc. Ch 1, turn.

Row 14:
Rep Row 4.

Row 15:
Sc in first 2 sc, (pebble st in next sc, sc in next sc) 3 times; *† split CT (see Pattern Stitches) around next 2 CTs on 2nd row below †; on working row, (sc in next sc, pebble st in next sc) 5 times; sc in next sc; rep from * 11 times more, then rep from † to † once; on working row, (sc in next sc, pebble st in next sc) 3 times; sc in next 2 sc. Ch 1, turn.

Row 16:
Rep Row 4.

Row 17:
Sc in first sc; (pebble st in next sc, sc in next sc) 3 times; *† CT around next CT on 2nd row below; on working row, sc in next sc, CT around same CT as last CT made on 2nd row below †; on working row, (sc in next sc, pebble st in next sc) 4 times; sc in next sc; rep from * 11 times more, then rep from † to † once; on working row, (sc in next sc, pebble st in next sc) 3 times; sc in next sc. Ch 1, turn.

Row 18:
Rep Row 4.

Row 19:
Rep Row 11.

Row 20:
Rep Row 4.

Row 21:
Rep Row 9.

Row 22:
Rep Row 4.

Row 23:
Rep Row 7.

Row 24:
Rep Row 4.

Row 25:
Sc in first sc, pebble st in next sc; sc in next sc, CT around next CT on 2nd row below; *† on working row, (sc in next sc, pebble st in next sc) 4 times; sc in next sc †; CT around next CT on 2nd row below; on working row, sc in next sc, CT around next CT on 2nd row below; rep from * 11 times more, then rep from † to † once; CT around next CT on 2nd row below; on working row, sc in next sc, pebble st in next sc; sc in next sc. Ch 1, turn.

Row 26:
Rep Row 4.

Row 27:
Sc in first 2 sc, CT around next CT on 2nd row below; *† on working row, (sc in next sc, pebble st in next sc) 5 times; sc in next sc †; split CT around next 2 CTs on 2nd row below; rep from * 11 times more, then rep from † to † once; CT around next CT on 2nd row below; on working row, sc in next 2 sc. Ch 1, turn.

Rep Rows 4 through 27 until piece measures about 60", ending by working a Row 27. At end of last row, do not ch 1.

Finish off and weave in all ends.

Fringe

Following Fringe instructions on page 159, make Triple Knot Fringe. Cut 30" strands; use 8 strands for each knot. Working across each short end of afghan, tie knots evenly spaced (about every 3rd st). Trim ends even.

Sonata *designed by Ann Kirtley*

Size:
About 52" x 83"

Materials:
Worsted weight yarn, 79 oz (5530 yds, 2370 gms) off white

Note: Our photographed afghan was made with Red Heart® Super Saver, Aran #313.

Size F (3.75mm) crochet hook, or size required for gauge
Size 16 tapestry needle

Gauge:
In pattern:
3 pattern reps = 6"
6 rows = 3"

Pattern Stitches

Back Post Double Crochet (BPdc):
YO, insert hook from back to front to back around post (see Stitch Guide on page 160) of st indicated, draw lp through, (YO, draw through 2 lps on hook) twice—BPdc made.

Front Post Double Crochet (FPdc):
YO, insert hook from front to back to front around post (see Stitch Guide on page 160) of st indicated, draw lp through, (YO, draw through 2 lps on hook) twice—FPdc made.

Cable Stitch (cable st):
Ch 3, drop lp from hook, insert hook in sp indicated, insert hook in dropped lp and pull to front, YO, draw through lp on hook—cable st made.

Popcorn (PC):
5 dc in st indicated; drop lp, insert hook in first dc made, draw dropped lp through—PC made.

Cascading petals border this most elegant of afghans. Created in off-white, its romantic style is lovely for wedding and anniversary gifting.

Instructions

Center
Ch 148.

Row 1 (right side):
Dc in 4th ch from hook (beg 3 skipped chs count as a dc); * sk next 3 chs, in next ch work (3 dc, ch 1, 3 dc); sk next 3 chs, dc in next 2 chs; rep from * 18 times more. Ch 4 (counts as first dc and ch-1 sp on following rows), turn.

continued

Sonata

Row 2:
Dc in first dc, ch 1, BPdc (see Pattern Stitches on page 103) around next dc; sk next 3 dc, sc in next ch-1 sp, sk next 3 dc, BPdc around next dc, ch 1; * in sp between last dc worked and next dc work (dc, ch 1, dc); ch 1, BPdc around next dc; sk next 3 dc, sc in next ch-1 sp; sk next 3 dc, BPdc around next dc; ch 1; rep from * 18 times more; dc in sp between last dc worked and beg 3 skipped chs, ch 1, dc in 3rd ch of beg 3 skipped chs. Ch 4, turn.

Row 3:
2 dc in next ch-1 sp, FPdc (see Pattern Stitches on page 103) around each of next 2 BPdc; sk next ch-1 sp; * in next ch-1 sp work (2 dc, ch 3, 2 dc); FPdc around each of next 2 BPdc; sk next ch-1 sp; rep from * 18 times more; 2 dc in sp formed by turning ch; ch 1, dc in 3rd ch of same turning ch. Ch 4, turn.

Row 4:
3 dc in next ch-1 sp; BPdc around each of next 2 FPdc; * in next ch-3 sp work (3 dc, ch 1, 3 dc); BPdc around each of next 2 FPdc; rep from * 18 times more; 3 dc in sp formed by turning ch; ch 1, dc in 3rd ch of same turning ch. Ch 1, turn.

Row 5:
Sc in first dc; * sc in next ch-1 sp, FPdc around next BPdc; ch 1, in sp between last dc worked and next dc work (dc, ch 1, dc); ch 1, FPdc around next BPdc; rep from * 18 times more; sc in sp formed by turning ch and in 3rd ch of same turning ch. Ch 3 (counts as first dc on following rows), turn.

Row 6:
* BPdc around next FPdc; sk next ch-1 sp, in next ch-1 sp work (2 dc, ch 3, 2 dc); BPdc around next FPdc; rep from * 18 times more; sk next sc, dc in next sc. Ch 3, turn.

Row 7:
* FPdc around next BPdc; in next ch-3 sp work (3 dc, ch 1, 3 dc); FPdc around next BPdc; rep from * 18 times more; dc in 3rd ch of turning ch-3. Ch 4, turn.

Row 8:
Dc in first dc, ch 1, BPdc around next FPdc; sc in next ch-1 sp, BPdc around next FPdc; ch 1; * in sp between last dc worked and next dc work (dc, ch 1, dc); ch 1, BPdc around next FPdc; sc in next ch-1 sp, BPdc around next FPdc; ch 1; rep from * 18 times more; in 3rd ch of turning ch-3 work (dc, ch 1, dc). Ch 4, turn.

Rows 9 through 152:
Rep Rows 3 through 8 twenty-four times more. At end of Row 152, do not ch 4. Finish off.

Edging
Ch 35.

Row 1 (wrong side):
Sc in 2nd ch from hook and in next 2 chs; ch 5, (sk next 4 chs, sc in next ch, ch 5) 5 times; sk next 5 chs, in next ch work (3 dc, ch 2, 3 dc)—shell made. Ch 5, turn.

Row 2 (right side):
In ch-2 sp of next shell work shell; work petal (to work petal: ch 12, sc in 2nd ch from hook, hdc in next ch, dc in next ch, trc in next ch, 2 trc in next ch; trc in next ch, dc in next 2 chs, hdc in next ch, sc in next ch, sl st in next ch, working along opposite side in unused lps of ch-12, sl st in first lp, sc in next lp, hdc in next lp, dc in next 2 lps, trc in next lp, 2 trc in next lp; trc in next lp, dc in next lp, hdc in next lp, sc in next lp, sl st in next lp—petal made); sk next ch-5 sp, in next ch-5 sp work (sc, petal); sk next ch-5 sp, shell in next ch-5 sp; ch 5, sk next ch-5 sp, sc in next ch-5 sp, ch 5, sl st in next 3 sc. Ch 9, turn.

Row 3:
(Sc in next ch-5 sp, ch 5) twice; shell in next shell; ch 11, sc in sc between petals, ch 11, shell in next shell. Ch 5, turn.

Row 4:
Shell in next shell; in next ch-11 sp work 6 cable sts (see Pattern Stitches on page 103); ch 3, PC (see Pattern Stitches on page 103) in next sc; in next ch-11 sp work 6 cable sts; ch 3, shell in next shell; ch 5, (sc in next ch-5 sp, ch 5) twice; sk first 2 chs of turning ch, sc in next 3 chs. Ch 9, turn.

Row 5:
(Sc in next ch-5 sp, ch 5) 3 times; shell in next shell; ch 5, sc in next ch-11 sp between 3rd and 4th cable sts, ch 5, sl st in next PC, ch 5, sc in next ch-11 sp between 3rd and 4th cable sts, ch 5, shell in next shell. Ch 5, turn.

Row 6:
Shell in next shell; work petal; sl st in FL of 3rd dc of next PC on 2nd row below, work petal; shell in next shell; ch 5, (sc in next ch-5 sp, ch 5) 3 times; sk first 2 chs of turning ch, sc in next 3 chs. Ch 9, turn.

Row 7:
(Sc in next ch-5 sp, ch 5) 4 times; shell in next shell; ch 5, sc in 3rd trc of next petal, ch 5, sc in sl st between petals, ch 5, sc in 3rd trc of next petal, shell in next shell. Ch 5, turn.

Row 8:
* Shell in next shell; ch 5, (sc in next ch-5 sp, ch 5) 4 times; rep from * once more; sk first 2 chs of turning ch, sc in next 3 chs. Ch 9, turn.

Row 9:
(Sc in next ch-5 sp, ch 5) 5 times; shell in next shell; ch 5, sk next ch-5 sp, (sc in next ch-5 sp, ch 5) 3 times; sk next ch-5 sp, shell in next shell. Ch 5, turn.

Row 10:
Shell in next shell; ch 5, sk next ch-5 sp, (sc in next ch-5 sp, ch 5) twice; sk next ch-5 sp, shell in next shell; ch 5, (sc in next ch-5 sp, ch 5) 5 times; sk first 2 chs of turning ch, sc in next 3 chs. Ch 9, turn.

Row 11:
(Sc in next ch-5 sp, ch 5) 6 times; shell in next shell; ch 5, sk next ch-5 sp, sc in next ch-5 sp, ch 5, sk next ch-5 sp, shell in next shell. Turn.

Row 12:
Sk first dc, sl st in next 2 dc, sc in next ch-2 sp, sk next 2 ch-5 sps, shell in next shell; ch 5, (sc in next ch-5 sp, ch 5) 6 times; sk first 2 chs of turning ch, sc in next 3 chs. Ch 9, turn.

Row 13:
(Sc in next ch-5 sp, ch 5) twice; shell in next ch-5 sp; ch 5, sk next ch-5 sp, (sc in next ch-5 sp, ch 5) twice; sk next ch-5 sp, shell in next shell. Ch 5, leaving rem sts unworked.

Row 14:
Shell in next shell; work petal; sk next ch-5 sp, sc in next ch-5 sp, work petal; sk next ch-5 sp, shell in next shell; ch 5, sk next ch-5 sp, sc in next ch-5 sp, ch 5, sk first 2 chs of turning ch, sc in next 3 chs. Ch 9, turn.

Rows 15 through 62:
Rep Rows 3 through 14 four times more.

Rows 63 through 66:
Rep Rows 3 through 6. At end of Row 66, do not ch 9. Ch 8, turn.

Rows 67 and 68:
Rep Rows 7 and 8. At end of Row 68, do not ch 9. Ch 8, turn.

Rows 69 and 70:
Rep Rows 9 and 10. At end of Row 70, do not ch 9. Ch 8, turn.

Rows 71 and 72:
Rep Rows 11 and 12. At end of Row 72, do not ch 9. Ch 8, turn.

Rows 73 and 74:
Rep Rows 13 and 14. At end of Row 74, do not ch 9. Ch 8, turn.

Rows 75 and 76:
Rep Rows 3 and 4. At end of Row 76, do not ch 9. Ch 7, turn.

Rows 77 and 78:
Rep Rows 5 and 6. At end of Row 78, do not ch 9. Ch 7, turn.

Rows 79 and 80:
Rep Rows 7 and 8. At end of Row 80, do not ch 9. Ch 7, turn.

Rows 81 and 82:
Rep Rows 9 and 10. At end of Row 82, do not ch 9. Ch 7, turn.

Rows 83 and 84:
Rep Rows 11 and 12. At end of Row 84, do not ch 9. Ch 7, turn.

Row 85:
(Sc in next ch-5 sp, ch 5) 6 times; sk next ch-5 sp, shell in next shell. Ch 5, leaving rem sts unworked.

Row 86:
Sc in ch-2 sp of next shell, ch 5, (sc in next ch-5 sp, ch 5) 6 times; sk first 2 chs of turning ch, sc in next 3 chs. Ch 6, turn.

Row 87:
(Sc in next ch-5 sp, ch 5) 7 times; sc in sp formed by turning ch. Ch 5, turn.

Row 88:
(Sc in next ch-5 sp, ch 5) 6 times; sc in next ch-5 sp. Ch 5, turn, leaving sp formed by turning ch unworked.

Row 89:
(Sc in next ch-5 sp, ch 5) 6 times; sc in sp formed by turning ch. Ch 5, turn.

Rows 90 and 91:
Rep Row 89.

Row 92:
(Sc in next ch-5 sp, ch 5) 6 times; sc in sp formed by turning ch, ch 5; working along side edge, sc in sp formed by next turning ch, ch 5, sk first 2 chs of next turning ch, sc in next 3 chs. Ch 6, turn.

Row 93:
(Sc in next ch-5 sp, ch 5) 6 times; sc in next ch-5 sp. Ch 5, turn, leaving rem ch-5 sps unworked.

Row 94:
Shell in next ch-5 sp; work petal; sk next ch-5 sp, sc in next ch-5 sp, work petal; sk next ch-5 sp, shell in next ch-5 sp; ch 5, sc in next ch-5 sp, ch 5, sk first 2 chs of turning ch, sc in next 3 chs. Ch 6, turn.

Rows 95 and 96:
Rep Rows 3 and 4. At end of Row 96, do not ch 9. Ch 7, turn.

Rows 97 and 98:
Rep Rows 5 and 6. At end of Row 98, do not ch 9. Ch 7, turn.

Rows 99 and 100:
Rep Rows 7 and 8. At end of Row 100, do not ch 9. Ch 7, turn.

Rows 101 and 102:
Rep Rows 9 and 10. At end of Row 102, do not ch 9. Ch 7, turn.

Rows 103 and 104:
Rep Rows 11 and 12. At end of Row 104, do not ch 9. Ch 7, turn.

continued

Sonata

Rows 105 and 106:
Rep Rows 13 and 14. At end of Row 106, do not ch 9. Ch 8, turn.

Rows 107 and 108:
Rep Rows 3 and 4. At end of Row 108, do not ch 9. Ch 8, turn.

Rows 109 and 110:
Rep Rows 5 and 6. At end of Row 110, do not ch 9. Ch 8, turn.

Rows 111 through 118:
Rep Rows 7 through 14.

Rows 119 through 130:
Rep Rows 3 through 14.

Rows 131 through 186:
Rep Rows 63 through 118.

Rows 187 through 234:
Rep Rows 3 through 14 four times.

Rows 235 through 290:
Rep Rows 63 through 118.

Rows 291 through 302:
Rep Rows 3 through 14.

Rows 303 through 344:
Rep Rows 63 through 104. At end of Row 344, ch 4, turn.

Note: *Following row joins end of edging to beginning of edging. Check edging carefully before joining so that it is not twisted.*

Row 345 (joining row):
Hold right side of beg ch of edging facing right side of working end; working across beg ch of edging, sl st in unused lps of first 3 chs; on working row, sl st in next 2 chs of next ch-5 sp; * sc in same sp and in next sp formed by skipped chs of beg ch at same time; on working row, sl st in last 2 chs of same ch-5 sp, in next sc, and in first 2 chs of next ch-5 sp; rep from * 4 times more; sc in same sp and in next sp formed by skipped chs of beg ch at same time; on working row, sl st in last 2 chs of same ch-5 sp, in next sc, in next 5 chs of next ch-5 sp, and in next 3 dc; sl st in next ch-2 sp and in unused lp of beg ch at base of shell at same time. Finish off.

Edging:

Note: *Edging is worked along side of border. On border when working sc in ch-2 sp of shell, work sc to right of dc previously worked in same sp.*

Hold edging with right side facing you and Row 12 at top; sk first sc of Row 12, join in first dc of next shell on same row; ch 1, sc in same dc; * sk next 2 dc, sc in next ch-2 sp, ch 3, dc in 3rd ch from hook; † in turning ch-5 sp of next row work (sc, ch 3, dc in 3rd ch from hook) twice; sc in ch-2 sp of next shell on same row, ch 3, dc in 3rd ch from hook †; rep from † to † 4 times more; sc in first sl st of next row, ch 3, dc in 3rd ch from hook; sc in first dc of next shell on same row; rep from * 5 times more; sc in ch-2 sp of same shell, ch 3, dc in 3rd ch from hook; sc in first ch of next turning ch, ch 3, dc in 3rd ch from hook; (sc in side of next sc, ch 3, dc in 3rd ch from hook) 3 times; (sc in next sc, ch 3, dc in 3rd ch from hook) twice; sc in side of next sc, ch 3, dc in 3rd ch from hook; in next turning ch work (sc, ch 3, dc in 3rd ch from hook) twice; sc in next ch-2 sp, ch 3, dc in 3rd ch from hook; rep from † to † 4 times; sc in first sl st of next row, ch 3, dc in 3rd ch from hook; sk next sc, sc in first dc of next shell; sk next 2 dc, sc in next ch-2 sp, ch 3, dc in 3rd ch from hook; rep from † to † 5 times; sc in first sl st of next row, ch 3, dc in 3rd ch from hook; sc in first dc of next shell on same row; sc in ch-2 sp of same shell, ch 3, dc in 3rd ch from hook; sc in first ch of next turning ch, ch 3, dc in 3rd ch from hook; (sc in side of next sc, ch 3, dc in 3rd ch from hook) 3 times; (sc in next sc, ch 3, dc in 3rd ch from hook) twice; sc in side of next sc, ch 3, dc in 3rd ch from hook, in next turning ch work (sc, ch 3, dc in 3rd ch from hook) twice; sc in next ch-2 sp, ch 3, dc in 3rd ch from hook; rep from † to † 4 times; sc in first sl st of next row, ch 3, dc in 3rd ch from hook; sk next sc, sc in first dc of next shell on same row; †† sk next 2 dc, sc in next ch-2 sp, ch 3, dc in 3rd ch from hook; rep from † to † 5 times; sc in first sl st of next row, ch 3, dc in 3rd ch from hook; sc in first dc of next shell on same row ††; rep from †† to †† 6 times more; sc in ch-2 sp of same shell, ch 3, dc in 3rd ch from hook; sc in first ch of next turning ch, ch 3, dc in 3rd ch from hook; (sc in side of next sc, ch 3, dc in 3rd ch from hook) 3 times; (sc in next sc, ch 3, dc in 3rd ch from hook) twice; sc in side of next sc, ch 3, dc in 3rd ch from hook; in next turning ch work (sc, ch 3, dc in 3rd ch from hook) twice; sc in next ch-2 sp, ch 3, dc in 3rd ch from hook; rep from † to † 4 times; sc in first sl st of next row, ch 3, dc in 3rd ch from hook; sk next sc, sc in first dc of next shell; rep from †† to †† 4 times; sc in ch-2 sp of same shell, ch 3, dc in 3rd ch from hook; in next turning ch work (sc, ch 3, dc in 3rd ch from hook) twice; (sc in side of next sc, ch 3, dc in 3rd ch from hook) 3 times; (sc in next sc, ch 3, dc in 3rd ch from hook) twice; sc in side of next sc, ch 3, dc in 3rd ch from hook, rep from † to † 5 times; sc in first sl st of next row, ch 3, dc in 3rd ch from hook; sc in first dc of next shell on same row, sk next 2 dc, sc in next ch-2 sp, ch 3, dc in 3rd ch from hook; rep from † to † 5 times; sc in first sl st of next row, ch 3, dc in 3rd ch from hook; join in first sc.

Finish off and weave in ends.

Assembly

Place edging around outside of center and pin in place, carefully matching corner sts on border to corners on center. With tapestry needle and yarn, sew edging to body from wrong side.

Spanish Tiles designed by Kathleen Garen

This Southwestern-style throw is worked side to side, carrying colors that create the design. Ends are not woven in, but rather knotted and left long to form fringe.

Spanish Tiles

Size:
About 37" x 48" before fringe

Materials:
Worsted weight yarn, 20 oz (1400 yds, 600 gms) yellow; 10 oz (700 yds, 300 gms) teal; 9 oz (630 yds, 270 gms) rust; 1 oz (70 yds, 30 gms) med brown

Note: *Our photographed afghan was made with Red Heart® Classic™, Cornmeal #220, Teal #48, Med. Clay #280 and Mid Brown #339.*

Size J (6mm) crochet hook, or size required for gauge
Size 16 tapestry needle

Gauge:
3 sc = 1"

Pattern Stitch

Long Double Crochet (long dc):
YO, insert hook in unused lp of st indicated on 2nd row below, (YO, draw through 2 lps on hook) twice—long dc made.

Instructions

Note: *Afghan is worked all on right side. Join a new strand of yarn for each row, leaving 12" yarn ends at sides. Yarn ends form fringe. To join new color at beginning of row, with new color make slip knot on hook and join with an sc.*

With yellow, ch 186.

Row 1 (right side):
Sc in 2nd ch from hook and in each rem ch—185 sc. Finish off.

Row 2:
Join yellow in BL of first sc; working in BLs only, sc in each rem sc. Finish off.

Row 3:
Rep Row 2.

Row 4:
Join yellow in BL of first sc; sc in BL of next sc; long dc (see Pattern Stitch) in next sc on 2nd row below; * on working row, sk next sc, sc in BLs of next 5 sc; long dc in next sc on 2nd row below; rep from * 29 times more; on working row, sk next sc, sc in BLs of next 2 sc. Finish off.

Row 5:
Rep Row 2.

Row 6:
Join yellow in BL of first sc; sc in BLs of next 2 sc; long dc in next sc on 2nd row below; * † on working row, sk next sc, sc in BLs of next 3 sc, long dc in next sc on 2nd row below; on working row, sk next sc, sc in BL of next sc †; long dc in next sc on 2nd row below; rep from * 28 times more, then rep from † to † once; on working row, sc in BLs of next 2 sc. Finish off.

Row 7:
Rep Row 2.

Row 8:
Join yellow in BL of first sc; sc in BLs of next 3 sc; * long dc in next sc on 2nd row below; on working row, sk next sc, sc in BL of next sc; long dc in next sc on 2nd row below; on working row, sk next sc, sc in BLs of next 3 sc; rep from * 29 times more; sc in BL of next sc. Finish off.

Row 9:
Rep Row 2.

Row 10:
Join yellow in BL of first sc; sc in BLs of next 4 sc, long dc in next sc on 2nd row below; * on working row, sk next sc, sc in BLs of next 5 sc, long dc in next sc on 2nd row below; rep from * 28 times more; on working row, sk next sc, sc in BLs of next 5 sc. Finish off.

Row 11:
Rep Row 2.

Row 12:
Join teal in BL of first sc; working in BLs only, sc in each rem sc. Finish off.

Row 13:
Join yellow in BL of first sc; sc in BL of next sc, long dc in each of next 2 sc on 2nd row below; on working row, sk next 2 sc, sc in BL of next sc, changing to rust; * † sc in BLs of next 8 sc, changing to yellow in last sc †; long dc in each of next 3 sc on 2nd row below; on working row, sk next 3 sc, sc in BL of next sc, changing to rust; rep from * 13 times more, then rep from † to † once; long dc in each of next 2 sc on 2nd row below; on working row, sk next 2 sc, sc in BLs of next 2 sc. Finish off.

Row 14:
Join teal in BL of first sc; sc in BLs of next 3 sc; * long dc in next st on 2nd row below; on working row, sk next sc, sc in BLs of next 7 sc, long dc in next st on 2nd row below; on working row, sk next sc, sc in BLs of next 3 sc; rep from * 14 times more; sc in next BL of next sc. Finish off.

Row 15:
Join rust in BL of first sc; sc in BLs of next 4 sts; * long dc in next st on 2nd row below; on working row, sk next st, sc in BLs of next 5 sts; rep from * across. Finish off.

Row 16:
Join teal in BL of first sc; sc in BL of next st, long dc in next st on 2nd row below; * on working row, sk next st, sc in BLs of next 3 sts, long dc in next st on 2nd row below; rep from * 44 times more; on working row, sk next st, sc in BLs of next 2 sts. Finish off.

Row 17:
Join rust in BL of first sc; sc in BLs of next 2 sts; * long dc in next st on 2nd row below; on working row, sk next st, sc in BLs of next 3 sts, long dc in each of next 3 sts on 2nd row below; on working row, sk next 3 sts, sc in BLs of next 3 sts, long dc in next st on 2nd row below; on working row, sk next st, sc in BL of next st; rep from * 14 times more; sc in BLs of next 2 sts. Finish off.

Row 18:
Join teal in BL of first sc; sc in BL of next st, long dc in next st on 2nd row below; * on working row, sk next st, sc in BL of next st, long dc in next st on 2nd row below; on working row, sk next st, sc in BL of next st, changing to med brown; sc in BL of next st, hdc in BLs of next 3 sts, sc in BL of next st, changing to teal; sc in BL of next st, long dc in next st on 2nd row below; on working row, sk next st, sc in BL of next st, long dc in next st on 2nd row below; rep from * 14 times more; on working row, sk next st, sc in BLs of next 2 sts. Finish off.

Row 19:
Join rust in BL of first sc; sc in BLs of next 2 sts; * long dc in next st on 2nd row below; on working row, sk next st, sc in BL of next st, long dc in each of next 2 sts on 2nd row below; on working row, sk next 2 sts, sc in BLs of next 3 sts, long dc in each of next 2 sts on 2nd row below; on working row, sk next 2 sts, sc in BL of next st, long dc in next st on 2nd row below; on working row, sk next st, sc in BL of next st; rep from * 14 times more; sc in BLs of next 2 sts. Finish off.

Row 20:
Join teal in BL of first sc; sc in BL of next st; * long dc in next st on 2nd row below; on working row, sk next st, sc in BL of next st, long dc in next st on 2nd row below; on working row, sk next st, sc in BLs of next 7 sts, long dc in next st on 2nd row below; on working row, sk next st, sc in BL of next st; rep from * 14 times more; long dc in next st on 2nd row below; on working row, sk next st, sc in BLs of next 2 sts. Finish off.

Row 21:
Rep Row 17.

Row 22:
Rep Row 16.

Row 23:
Join yellow in BL of first sc; * sc in BLs of next 3 sts, changing to rust in last sc; sc in BL of next st, long dc in next st on 2nd row below; on working row, sk next st, sc in BLs of next 5 sts, long dc in next st on 2nd row below, changing to yellow; on working row, sk next st, sc in BL of next st; rep from * 14 times more; sc in BLs of next 4 sts. Finish off.

Row 24:
Rep Row 14.

Row 25:
Join yellow in BL of first sc; sc in BL of next st, long dc in each of next 2 sts on 2nd row below; on working row, sk next 2 sts; * sc in BLs of next 9 sts, long dc in each of next 3 sts on 2nd row below; on working row, sk next 3 sts; rep from * 13 times more; sc in BLs of next 9 sts, long dc in each of next 2 sts on 2nd row below; on working row, sk next 2 sts, sc in BLs of next 2 sts. Finish off.

Rows 26 through 121:
Rep Rows 2 through 25 four times more.

Rows 122 through 131:
Rep Rows 2 through 11.

Row 132:
Rep Row 2.

Trim ends even.

Twilight Tapestry

designed by Eleanor Albano-Miles

This handsome afghan is fun-to-stitch with colorful variegated yarn. Each panel is worked side to side, with puff stitches forming the borders.

Size:
About 46" x 65"

Materials:
Worsted weight yarn, 18 oz (1260 yds, 540 gms) variegated; 10½ oz (735 yds, 315 gms) off white; 9 oz (630 yds, 270 gms) blue

Note: *Our photographed afghan was made with Caron® Sayelle®, Woodsy Ombre #1406, Lapis #2060 and Fisherman #336.*

Size J (6mm) crochet hook, or size required for gauge
Size 16 tapestry needle

Gauge:
3 sc = 1"

Pattern Stitch

Puff Stitch (puff st):
(YO, draw up lp in st indicated) twice; YO and draw through all 5 lps on hook—puff st made.

Instructions

Panel (make 4)

Center:
With variegated, ch 208.

Row 1 (right side):
In 7th ch from hook work (dc, ch 2, dc); * sk next 2 chs, in next ch work (dc, ch 2, dc); rep from * 65 times more; ch 1, sk next 2 chs, dc in next ch. Ch 4, turn.

Row 2:
In each ch-2 sp work (dc, ch 2, dc); ch 1, dc in 4th ch of beg 6 skipped chs. Ch 4, turn.

Row 3:
In each ch-2 sp work (dc, ch 2, dc); ch 1, dc in 3rd ch of turning ch-4. Ch 4, turn.

Rows 4 through 9:
Rep Row 3 six times more. At end of Row 9, do not ch 4. Finish off.

continued

Twilight Tapestry

Panel Border:
Hold panel with right side facing you and beg ch at bottom; join variegated in sp formed by turning ch-4 in upper right-hand corner.

Rnd 1 (right side):
Ch 2 (counts as an hdc), in same sp work (hdc, ch 2, 2 hdc)—beg corner made; * hdc in next dc, in next ch-2 sp, in next 2 dc, in next ch-2 sp, and in next dc; sk next dc, hdc in next ch-2 sp and in next dc; rep from * 21 times more; hdc in next dc, 2 hdc in next ch-2 sp; sk next dc, in next ch-1 sp work (2 hdc, ch 2, 2 hdc)—corner made; † working in ends of rows in sps formed by edge dc and turning chs, 2 hdc in each of next 2 rows; (hdc in next row, 2 hdc in next row) twice; hdc in next row †; in last row work (2 hdc, ch 2, 2 hdc)—corner made; working in sps formed by skipped chs and in unused lps of beg ch, †† (hdc in next lp, 2 hdc in next ch-2 sp) twice; hdc in next lp, hdc in next ch-2 sp ††; rep from †† to †† 20 times more; (hdc in next lp, 2 hdc in next ch-2 sp) 3 times; 2 hdc in next lp; in sp formed by beg skipped chs work (2 hdc, ch 2, 2 hdc)—corner made; rep from † to † once; join in 2nd ch of beg ch-2. Finish off.

Hold panel with right side facing you and beg ch at bottom; join off white in ch-2 sp in upper right-hand corner.

Rnd 2:
Ch 1, in same sp work [puff st (see Pattern Stitch on page 111), ch 2, puff st]—puff st corner made; * ch 1, sk next hdc; † (puff st in next hdc, ch 1, sk next hdc) †; rep from † to † across to next corner ch-2 sp; in corner ch-2 sp work (puff st, ch 2, puff st)—puff st corner made ; rep from * twice more; ch 1, sk next hdc; rep from † to † across to first puff st; join in first puff st. Finish off.

Hold panel with right side facing you; join blue in ch-2 sp in upper right-hand corner.

Rnd 3:
Ch 5 (counts as an hdc and ch-3 sp), hdc in same sp—beg hdc corner made; * hdc in each puff st and in each ch-1 sp to next corner ch-2 sp; in corner ch-2 sp work (hdc, ch 3, hdc)—hdc corner made; rep from * twice more; hdc in each puff st and in each ch-1 sp to beg ch-5; join in 2nd ch of beg ch-5.

Rnd 4:
Ch 2 (counts as an hdc on this and following rnds), in next ch-3 sp work hdc corner; * hdc in each hdc to next corner ch-3 sp; in corner ch-3 sp work hdc corner; rep from * twice more; hdc in each hdc to beg ch-2; join in 2nd ch of beg ch-2.

Rnd 5:
Ch 3 (counts as a dc), dc in next hdc, in next corner ch-3 sp work (dc, ch 3, dc)—dc corner made; * dc in each hdc to next corner ch-3 sp; in corner ch-3 sp work (dc, ch 3, dc)—dc corner made; rep from * twice more; dc in each hdc to beg ch-3; join in 3rd ch of beg ch-3. Finish off.

Hold panel with right side facing you and beg ch at bottom; join off white in ch-3 sp in upper right-hand corner.

Rnd 6:
Ch 1, in same sp work puff st corner; * ch 1, sk next dc; † (puff st in next dc, ch 1, sk next dc) †; rep from † to † across to next corner ch-3 sp; in corner ch-3 sp work puff st corner; rep from * twice more; ch 1, sk next dc; rep from † to † across to first puff st; join in first puff st.

Rnd 7:
Ch 2, in next corner ch-2 sp work hdc corner; * hdc in each puff st and in each ch-1 sp to next corner ch-2 sp; in corner ch-2 sp work hdc corner; rep from * twice more; hdc in each puff st and in each ch-1 sp to beg ch-2; join in 2nd ch of beg ch-2.

Finish off and weave in all ends.

Assembly

To join panels, hold two panels with right sides together and carefully matching stitches. With tapestry needle and off white, sew with overcast stitch (see Stitch Guide on page 160) through BLs only along one long side, beginning and ending in ch-3 sp of corners. Join remaining panels in same manner.

Border

Hold afghan with right side facing you and one short end at top; join off white in ch-3 sp in upper right-hand corner.

Rnd 1 (right side):
Ch 1, 3 sc in same sp—corner made; † sc in each sc to next ch-3 sp, hdc in ch-3 sp, dc in joining, hdc in next ch-3 sp †; rep from † to † twice more; sc in each sc to next corner ch-3 sp; in ch-3 sp work 3 sc—corner made; sc in each sc along next side to next corner ch-3 sp; in ch-3 sp work 3 sc—corner made; rep from † to † 3 times; sc in each sc to next corner ch-3 sp; in ch-3 sp work 3 sc—corner made; sc in each sc along next side to first sc; join in first sc.

Rnd 2:
Ch 1, sc in same sc; 3 sc in next sc; * sc in each sc to 2nd sc of next corner; 3 sc in 2nd sc; rep from * twice more; sc in each sc to first sc; join in first sc.

Finish off and weave in all ends.

Country

*F*or down-home comfort and lively colorations, here's a group of afghans that will surely please. From little kitties, strawberries and watermelons to diamonds and pinwheels these are the kind of afghans that make a house a home.

Christmas Floral **114**
Diagonal Diamonds . . . **118**
Harmony **120**
Remember the Kittens . **123**
Pinwheel Roses **125**
Rainbow's End **128**
Strawberry Jam **131**
Watermelon Picnic **135**

Christmas Floral
designed by Mike Cates

Size:
About 48" x 60"

Materials:
Worsted weight yarn, 28 oz (1960 yds, 840 gms) white; 20 oz (1400 yds, 600 gms) dk green; 17 oz (1190 yds, 510 gms) lt green; 7 oz (490 yds, 210 gms) red

Note: *Our photographed afghan was made with Red Heart® Classic™, White #001, Dk Sage #633, Lt Sage #631, and Cherry Red #912.*

Size H (5mm) crochet hook, or size required for gauge
Size 16 tapestry needle

Gauge:
one square = 7"

Pattern Stitches

Long Double Crochet (long dc):
YO, insert hook in sp indicated, draw up lp to height of working rnd, (YO, draw through 2 lps on hook) twice—long dc made.

Front Post Single Crochet (FPsc):
Insert hook from front to back to front around post (see Stitch Guide on page 160) of st indicated, draw up lp, YO and draw through 2 lps on hook—FPsc made.

Instructions

Note: *To change color, work until 2 lps of last st remain on hook (3 lps for an hdc). With new color, YO and draw through 2 lps on hook (3 lps for an hdc); cut old color unless otherwise specified.*

Square (make 50)
With red, ch 8; join to form a ring.

Rnd 1 (right side):
Ch 1, sc in ring; ch 4, (sc in ring, ch 4) 7 times; join in first sc. Change to white by drawing lp through; cut red.

Rnd 2:
Ch 1, sc in same sc; * ch 1, working behind ch-4 lps of Rnd 1, long dc (see Pattern Stitches) in ring between next 2 sc; ch 1, on working rnd, sc in next sc; rep from * 6 times more; ch 1, working behind ch-4 lps of Rnd 1, long dc in ring between next 2 sc, ch 1; join in first sc.

Rnd 3:
Ch 1, sc in same sc, in each ch-1 sp, and in each st, changing to red in last sc; join in first sc—32 sc.

Squares and triangles combine for this lush afghan you'll enjoy all winter long. Rather than the usual square or rectangle shaped afghan, the Christmas Floral has rounded edges and is finished with a crisscross, intertwined edging.

continued

Christmas Floral

Rnd 4:
Ch 1, sc in same sc; ch 5; * sk next sc, sc in next 3 sc, ch 5; rep from * 6 times more; sk next sc, sc in next 2 sc; join in first sc. Finish off.

Rnd 5:
Join white in 2nd sc of any 3-sc group; ch 1, sc in same sc; ch 1, working behind ch-5 lps of Rnd 4, 3 dc in unused sc on Rnd 3; ch 1, on working rnd, sk next sc, sc in next sc; * † ch 1, 3 dc in next unused sc on Rnd 3; ch 1 †; on working rnd, sk next sc, sc in next sc; rep from * 5 times more, then rep from † to † once; join in first sc.

Rnd 6:
Ch 1, sc in same sc, in each ch-1 sp, and in each st, changing to lt green in last sc; join in first sc—48 sc.

Rnd 7:
Ch 1, sc in same sc; ch 6; * sk next 2 sc, sc in next sc, ch 6; rep from * 14 times more; join in first sc. Finish off.

Rnd 8:
Working behind ch-6 lps on Rnd 7, join dk green in first skipped sc to left of rnd joining; ch 3 (counts as a dc), dc in same sc as joining; working behind ch-6 lps on Rnd 7, 2 dc in each skipped sc on Rnd 6, changing to white in last dc; join in 3rd ch of beg ch-3—64 dc.

Rnd 9:
Ch 2 (counts as an hdc on this and following rnds), sc in next 2 dc; * hdc in next 2 dc, sc in next 2 dc; rep from * 14 times more; hdc in next dc, changing to lt green; join in 2nd ch of beg ch-2.

Rnd 10:
Ch 2, hdc in next st; * † dc in next 2 sts, 2 trc in next st; ch 3, 2 trc in next st; dc in next 2 sts, hdc in next 2 sts, sc in next 6 sts †; hdc in next 2 sts; rep from * twice more, then rep from † to † once; join in 2nd ch of beg ch-2. Finish off.

Rnd 11:
Join dk green in any ch-3 sp, ch 1, in same sp work (sc, hdc, dc, hdc, sc)—corner made; sc in next 18 sts; * in next ch-3 sp work (sc, hdc, dc, hdc, sc)—corner made; sc in next 18 sts; rep from * twice more; join in first sc. Finish off and weave in all ends.

Triangle (make 18)
With white, ch 6.

Foundation Row (wrong side):
Sc in 2nd ch from hook, dc in next ch, ch 1, in next ch work (trc, ch 1, trc)—point made; ch 1, dc in next ch, sc in next ch. Ch 1, turn.

Note: Remainder of triangle is worked in rnds.

Rnd 1 (right side):
2 sc in first sc; sc in next dc, in next ch-1 sp, and in next trc; in next ch-1 sp work (hdc, dc, hdc); sc in next trc, in next ch-1 sp, and in next dc; in next sc work (2 sc, ch 3, sc); working on opposite side of beg ch, 2 sc in sp between sc just worked and next dc; sc in sp between next dc and next trc; sc in sp between next 2 trc, sc in sp between next trc and next dc, 2 sc in sp between next dc and next sc; sc in unused lp of next sc, ch 3; join in first sc. Finish off.

Rnd 2:
Hold piece with right side and point at bottom; join dk green in upper right-hand ch-3 sp; ch 1, 2 sc in same sp (mark first sc made); sc in next 9 sts, 2 sc in next ch-3 sp (mark last sc made); ch 5, sc in next 6 sts, in next dc work (hdc, dc, hdc); sc in next 6 sts, ch 5; join in first sc. Change to white by drawing lp through; cut dk green.

Rnd 3:
Ch 1, sc in same sc and in next 12 sts, in next ch-5 sp work (sc, hdc, dc, hdc, 2 sc); sc in next 7 sts, in next st work (hdc, dc, hdc)—point made; sc in next 7 sts, in next ch-5 sp work (2 sc, hdc, dc, hdc, sc); join in first sc. Finish off.

Rnd 4:
Join lt green in first sc to left of joining on prev rnd; ch 2 (counts as an hdc), hdc in next 2 sts, sc in next 7 sts, hdc in next 5 sts, in next st work (hdc, dc, ch 4, dc, hdc); sc in next 3 sts, hdc in next 8 sts, in next st work (dc, ch 4, dc); hdc in next 8 sts, sc in next 3 sts, in next st work (hdc, dc, ch 4, dc, hdc); hdc in next 2 sts; join in 2nd ch of beg ch-2. Change to dk green by drawing lp through; cut lt green.

Rnd 5:
Ch 1, sc in same ch as joining and in next 16 sts, in next ch-4 sp work (sc, hdc, ch 1, dc, ch 1, hdc, sc); (sc in next 2 sts, 2 sc in next st) 3 times; sc in next 5 sts, in next ch-4 sp work (sc, hdc, dc, hdc, sc); sc in next 5 sts, (2 sc in next st, sc in next 2 sts) 3 times; in next ch-4 sp work (sc, hdc, ch 1, dc, ch 1, hdc, sc); sc in next 4 sts; join in first sc. Finish off.

Trim Rows:

Row 1:
Hold piece with right side facing you and point at top; with red make slip knot on hook and join with a FPsc (see Pattern Stitches on page 115) around post of 9th st on Rnd 2; ch 5, FPsc around first sc on foundation row; ch 5, FPsc around post of first trc on foundation row; ch 5, FPsc around post of next trc on foundation row; ch 5, FPsc around post of next sc on foundation row; ch 5, FPsc around post of 5th st on Rnd 2. Finish off.

Row 2:
Hold piece with right side facing you and point at top; with lt green make slip knot on hook and join with a FPsc around marked sc in lower right-hand corner on Rnd 2; ch 6, on Rnd 1, sk next ch-3 sp and next sc, FPsc around next sc; ch 6, sk next 2 sc, FPsc around next sc; ch 6; sk next 3 sts, FPsc around next st; ch 6, sk next 2 sts, FPsc around next st; ch 6, FPsc around marked sc on Rnd 2.

Finish off and weave in all ends.

Assembly

Referring to **Layout** for placement, join squares and triangles. To join, hold two squares with right sides together and carefully matching stitches. Wth tapestry needle and dk green, sew with overcast stitch (see Stitch Guide on page 160) along one side, beginning and ending in corner dc. Join remaining squares and triangles in same manner, being sure all four-corner junctions are firmly joined.

Border

Hold afghan with right side facing you and one short end at top; with dk green make slip knot on hook and join with an sc in first st on first triangle in upper right-hand corner (see **Layout**).

Rnd 1 (right side):
Sc in next 24 sc, dc in next joining, (sc in next 25 sc, dc in next joining) twice; sc in next 25 sc, hdc in next joining; sc in next 22 sc, hdc in next joining; † (sc in next 25 sc, dc in next joining) 4 times; sc in next 25 sc, hdc in next joining; sc in next 22 sc, hdc in next joining †; (sc in next 25 sc, dc in next joining) 3 times; sc in next 25 sc, hdc in next joining, sc in next 22 sc, hdc in next joining; rep from † to † once; join in first sc. Change to red by drawing lp through; cut dk green.

Rnd 2:
Ch 1, sc in same sc; * ch 3, sk next sc, sc in next sc; rep from * to last sc; sk last sc; join in first sc. Finish off.

Rnd 3:
Working behind ch-3 sps, with lt green make slip knot on hook and join with an sc in any skipped sc on Rnd 1; ch 4; * working in front of next ch-3 sp, sc in next skipped sc, ch 4, working behind ch-3 sps, sc in next skipped sc on Rnd 1; ch 4; rep from * around; join in first sc.

Finish off and weave in all ends.

Layout

Start border here

Diagonal Diamonds
designed by Mary Thomas

Choose a vibrant shade of yarn and crochet this interesting stitch. You'll have a whole afghan of faceted diamonds before you know it.

Size:
About 40" x 60" before fringe

Materials:
Worsted weight yarn, 52 oz (3640 yds, 1560 gms) peach
Note: *Our photographed afghan was made with Red Heart® Classic™, Medium Coral #252.*
Size K (5mm) crochet hook, or size required for gauge
Size 16 tapestry needle

Gauge:
5 dc = 2"

Instructions
Note: *Afghan is worked with 2 strands of yarn held together.*
With 2 strands of yarn, ch 134 loosely.

Row 1:
Sc in 2nd ch from hook and in next 4 chs; * ch 5, sk next 3 chs, sc in next 5 chs; rep from * 15 times more—16 ch-5 sps. Ch 1, turn.

Row 2:
Sc in first 4 sc, ch 3, sk next sc, sc in next ch-5 sp, ch 3, sk next sc; * sc in next 3 sc, ch 3, sk next sc, sc in next ch-5 sp, ch 3, sk next sc; rep from * 14 times more; sc in next 4 sc—32 ch-3 sps. Ch 1, turn.

Row 3:
Sc in first 3 sc; * ch 3, sk next sc, sc in next ch-3 sp, in next sc, and in next ch-3 sp; ch 3, sk next sc, sc in next sc; * rep from * 15 times more; sc in next 2 sc. Ch 3, turn.

Row 4:
Sk first sc, dc in next sc, ch 3, sk next sc, sc in next ch-3 sp, in next 3 sc, and in next ch-3 sp; * ch 5, sk next sc, sc in next ch-3 sp, in next 3 sc, and in next ch-3 sp; rep from * 14 times more; ch 3, sk next sc, dc in next 2 sc. Ch 1, turn.

Row 5:
Sc in first 2 dc and in next ch-3 sp; ch 3, sk next sc, sc in next 3 sc; * ch 3, sk next sc, sc in next ch-5 sp, ch 3, sk next sc, sc in next 3 sc; rep from * 14 times more; ch 3, sk next sc, sc in next ch-3 sp, in next dc, and in 3rd ch of turning ch-3. Ch 1, turn.

Row 6:
Sc in first 3 sc and in next ch-3 sp; ch 3, sk next sc, sc in next sc, ch 3, sk next sc; * sc in next ch-3 sp, in next sc, and in next ch-3 sp; ch 3, sk next sc, sc in next sc, ch 3, sk next sc; rep from * 15 times more; sc in next ch-3 sp and in next 3 sc. Ch 1, turn.

Row 7:
Sc in first 4 sc and in next ch-3 sp; * ch 5, sk next sc, sc in next ch-3 sp, in next 3 sc, and in next ch-3 sp; rep from * 15 times more; ch 5, sk next sc, sc in next ch-3 sp and in next 4 sc. Ch 1, turn.

Rep Rows 2 through 7 until piece measures about 64", ending by working a Row 6.

Next Row:
Sc in next 4 sc and in next ch-3 sp; * ch 3, sk next sc, sc in next ch-3 sp, in next 3 sc, and in next ch-3 sp; rep from * 15 times more; ch 3, sk next sc, sc in next ch-3 sp and in next 4 sc.

Finish off and weave in all ends.

Fringe
Following Fringe instructions on page 159, make Triple Knot Fringe. Cut 25" strands; use 8 strands for each knot of fringe. Working across each short end of afghan, tie knots evenly spaced (about every 4th st). Trim ends even.

Harmony
designed by Denise Black

Here's the perfect combination of variegated yarn and post stitch solid rows. This noteworthy afghan gets rave reviews from everyone.

Size:
About 45" x 60"

Materials:
Worsted weight yarn, 30 oz (2100 yds, 900 gms) off white; 21½ oz (1505 yds, 645 gms) variegated

Note: Our photographed model was made with Red Heart® Soft, New Aran #7313, and Water Lily #7966.

Size J (6mm) crochet hook, or size required for gauge
Size 16 tapestry needle

Gauge:
13 dc = 4"

Pattern Stitches

Front Post Triple Crochet (FPtrc):
YO twice, insert hook from front to back to front around post (see Stitch Guide on page 160) of st indicated, draw up lp, (YO, draw through 2 lps on hook) 3 times—FPtrc made.

Note: Always skip sc behind FPtrc.

Cross Stitch (X-st):
Sk next st, FPtrc around post of next st on 2nd row below, FPtrc around post of skipped st on 2nd row below—X-st made.

Note: Always skip sc behind FPtrc.

Instructions

Body
Note: When changing color, work until 2 lps of last st rem on hook. With new color, YO and draw through 2 lps on hook. Cut old color.

With off white, ch 150.

Row 1 (right side):
Sc in 2nd ch from hook and in each rem ch—149 sc. Ch 1, turn.

Row 2:
Sc in each sc, changing to variegated in last sc. Ch 1, turn.

Row 3:
Sc in each sc. Ch 1, turn.

Row 4:
Sc in each sc, changing to off white in last sc. Ch 1, turn.

continued

Harmony

Row 5:
Sc in first 2 sc; FPtrc **(see Pattern Stitches on page 121)** around next sc on 2nd row below; on working row, sc in next 2 sc; * FPtrc around next sc on 2nd row below; on working row, sc in next 2 sc; rep from * 48 times more. Ch 1, turn.

Row 6:
Sc in each st, changing to variegated in last sc. Ch 1, turn.

Rows 7 through 218:
Rep Rows 3 through 6 fifty-three times more. At end of last row, do not change color.

Border

Rnd 1 (right side):
3 sc in first sc—corner made; sc in each sc to last sc; 3 sc in last sc—corner made; working across next side in ends of rows, sk Row 218, sc in each row to beg ch; working across next side in unused lps of beg ch, 3 sc in first lp—corner made; sc in each lp to last lp; 3 sc in last lp—corner made; working across next side in ends of rows, sc in each row to last row; sk last row; join in first sc.

Rnd 2:
Ch 1, sc in same sc; in next sc work corner; * sc in each sc to 2nd sc of next corner; corner in next sc; rep from * twice more; sc in each sc to first sc; join in first sc.

Rnd 3:
Ch 1, sc in same sc and in next sc, corner in next sc; * sc in each sc to 2nd sc of next corner; corner in next sc; rep from * twice more; sc in each sc to first sc; join in first sc.

Rnd 4:
Sl st in next sc, ch 1, sc in same sc; sc in next sc, corner in next sc; † sc in next 2 sc, †† X-st **(see Pattern Sitches on page 121)** over next 2 sc on 2nd rnd below; on working rnd, sc in next sc ††; rep from †† to †† 49 times more; sc in next sc, corner in next sc; sc in next 2 sc †; rep from †† to †† 73 times; sc in next 2 sc, corner in next sc; rep from † to † once; rep from †† to †† 72 times; X-st over next 2 sc on 2nd rnd below; on working rnd, sc in next sl st; join in first sc.

Rnd 5:
Ch 1, sc in same sc and in next 2 sc, corner in next sc; * sc in each sc to 2nd sc of next corner, corner in next sc; rep from * twice more; sc in each sc to first sc; join in first sc.

Rnd 6:
Ch 1, sc in same sc and in next 3 sc, corner in next sc; * sc in each sc to 2nd sc of next corner, corner in next sc; rep from * twice more; sc in each sc to first sc; join in first sc.

Finish off and weave in all ends.

Remember the Kittens by Joan Kokaska

*W*e have had so many requests for the "Kitten" afghan that appeared in an out of print book that we published many years ago we decided to include it here. It is just as charming today as when it was first published.

Remember the Kittens

Size:
About 40" x 60" before fringe

Materials:
Worsted weight yarn, 22 oz (1540 yds, 630 gms) white; 6 oz (1120 yds, 458 gms) each, grey and black

Note: *Our photographed afghan was made with Red Heart® Classic™, White #1, Nickel #401, and Black #12.*

Size H (5mm) crochet hook, or size required for gauge
Size 16 tapestry needle

Gauge:
4 dc = 1"
4 shells = 5"

Pattern Stitch

Puff Stitch (puff st):
(YO, draw up lp in sp between last shell worked and next shell on 2nd row below) 4 times; YO, draw through 8 lps on hook, YO and draw through 2 rem lps on hook—puff st made.

Instructions

Note: *Afghan is reversible. To change colors, work until 2 lps of last st rem on hook. With new color, YO and draw 2 lps on hook; cut old color.*

With black, ch 164 loosely.

Row 1:
Dc in 4th ch from hook (beg 3 skipped chs count as a dc) and in next ch, ch 1, 2 dc in next ch; * sk next 3 chs, in next ch work (2 dc, ch 1, 2 dc)—shell made; rep from * 29 times more; sk next 2 chs, dc in next 2 chs—30 shells. Ch 3 (counts as first dc on following rows), turn.

Row 2:
Dc in next 2 dc, sk next 2 dc, shell in ch-1 sp of next shell; * sk next 4 dc, shell in ch-1 sp of next shell; rep from * 28 times more; sk next 2 dc, dc in next 2 dc and in 3rd ch of beg 3 skipped chs, changing to white in last dc. Ch 3, turn.

Row 3:
Dc in next 2 dc; * shell in next shell; puff st (see Pattern Stitch) in sp between last shell worked and next shell on 2nd row below; rep from * 28 times more; shell in next shell; sk next 2 dc, dc in next 2 dc and in 3rd ch of turning ch-3. Ch 3, turn.

Row 4:
Dc in next 2 dc, shell in each of next 30 shells; sk next 2 dc, dc in next 2 dc and in 3rd ch of turning ch-3. Ch 3, turn.

Row 5:
Dc in next 2 dc, shell in each of next 30 shells; sk next 2 dc, dc in next 2 dc and in 3rd ch of turning ch-3, changing to grey. Ch 3, turn.

Rows 6 through 8:
Rep Rows 3 through 5, changing to black at end of Row 8.

Rows 9 through 11:
Rep Rows 3 through 5, changing to white at end of Row 11.

Rep Rows 3 through 11 until piece measures about 60", ending by working a Row 10. At end of last row, do not ch 3.

Finish off and weave in all ends.

Fringe

Following Fringe instructions on page 159, make Single Knot Fringe. Cut 14" strands of white; use 12 strands for each knot. Working across each short end, tie one knot in each sp between shells and in sps at each end. Trim ends even.

Pinwheel Roses *designed by Diana Lynn Sippel*

This ingenious block features a clever way to join crocheted loops in the center forming the pinwheel flowers. You'll never get tired of this interesting design.

Pinwheel Roses

Size:
About 45" x 60"

Materials:
Worsted weight yarn, 13 oz (910 yds, 390 gms) black; 10 oz (700 yds, 300 gms) each, lt rose, med rose, and green; 7 oz (490 yds, 210 gms) dk rose

Note: *Our photographed afghan was made with Bernat® Silky Soft, Black #376, Medium Rose #362, Medium Green #359, Light Rose #361, and Dark Rose #363.*

Size G (4.25mm) crochet hook, or size required for gauge
Size 16 tapestry needle

Gauge:
4 sc = 1"

Pattern Stitch

Long Double Crochet (long dc):
YO, insert hook in sp indicated, draw up lp to height of working rnd, (YO, draw through 2 lps on hook) twice—long dc made.

Instructions

Petal (make 159 lt rose and 159 med rose)

Ch 12, sc in 2nd ch from hook and in next 2 chs, 2 hdc in next ch; 2 dc in each of next 2 chs; ch 1, 2 dc in each of next 2 chs; 2 hdc in next ch; sc in next 2 chs; join in first sc.

Finish off and weave in ends.

Motif (make 53)

Center Ring:
Stack petals with right sides up, starting with med rose and alternating lt rose and med rose until you have 6 petals in each stack (stack colors in same sequence for each motif).

With dk rose, ch 12. Slip beg ch-12 through center of one petal stack **(see photo)**; join to form a ring. **(Note:** Slide petals around ring as you work into beg ch. Petals should slide freely around center ring). Ch 3 **(counts as a dc)**, dc in same ch as joining; 2 dc in each rem ch; join in 3rd ch of beg ch-3.

Finish off and weave in ends.

Petal Joining:
With green make slip knot on hook and join with an sc in any ch-1 sp on any petal.

Rnd 1 (right side):
2 sc in same sp; * † sc in next 2 dc on working petal, ch 2; on next petal, sc in next 2 dc (before next ch-1 sp) †; 3 sc in next ch-1 sp; rep from * 4 times more, then rep from † to † once; join in first sc—42 sc.

Rnd 2:
Ch 1, sc in same sc; * 3 sc in next sc; sc in next 3 sc, 2 sc in next ch-2 sp; sc in next 3 sc; rep from * 5 times more; join in first sc—67 sc.

Rnd 3:
Ch 1, sc in same sc and in each rem sc; join in first sc. Change to black by drawing lp through; cut green.

Rnd 4:
Working over first 5 sc, work 5 long dc (see Pattern Stitch) in ch-1 sp of petal below; on working row, sc in next 6 sc; * working over next 5 sc on working row, 5 long dc in ch-1 sp of next petal; on working row, sc in next 6 sc; rep from * 4 times more; sk next sc; join in first long dc.

Rnd 5:
Ch 1, sc in same long dc and in next long dc; * 3 sc in next long dc—corner made; sc in next 2 long dc, in next 6 sc, and in next 2 long dc; rep from * 4 times more; 3 sc in next long dc—corner made; sc in next 2 long dc and in next 6 sc; join in first sc.

Finish off and weave in ends.

Assembly
Referring to **Layout** for placement, join motifs in 4 rows of 8 motifs each and 3 rows of 7 motifs each. To join motifs, hold 2 motifs with right sides together; with tapestry needle and black, sew together with overcast stitch (see Stitch Guide on page 160) along one side, beginning and ending with corner sc. Join motifs in rows and then sew rows together in same manner, being sure all four-corner junctions are firmly joined.

Border
Hold afghan with right side facing you and one short edge at top; with black make slip knot on hook and join with an sc in 2nd sc of corner indicated in **Layout**.

Rnd 1 (right side):
2 sc in same sc; sc in each sc to 2nd sc of next corner, * 3 sc in next corner; sc in each sc to 2nd sc of next corner; rep from * around; join in joining sc.

Rnd 2:
Ch 1, sc in same sc and in each rem sc; join in first sc.

Finish off and weave in all ends.

Layout

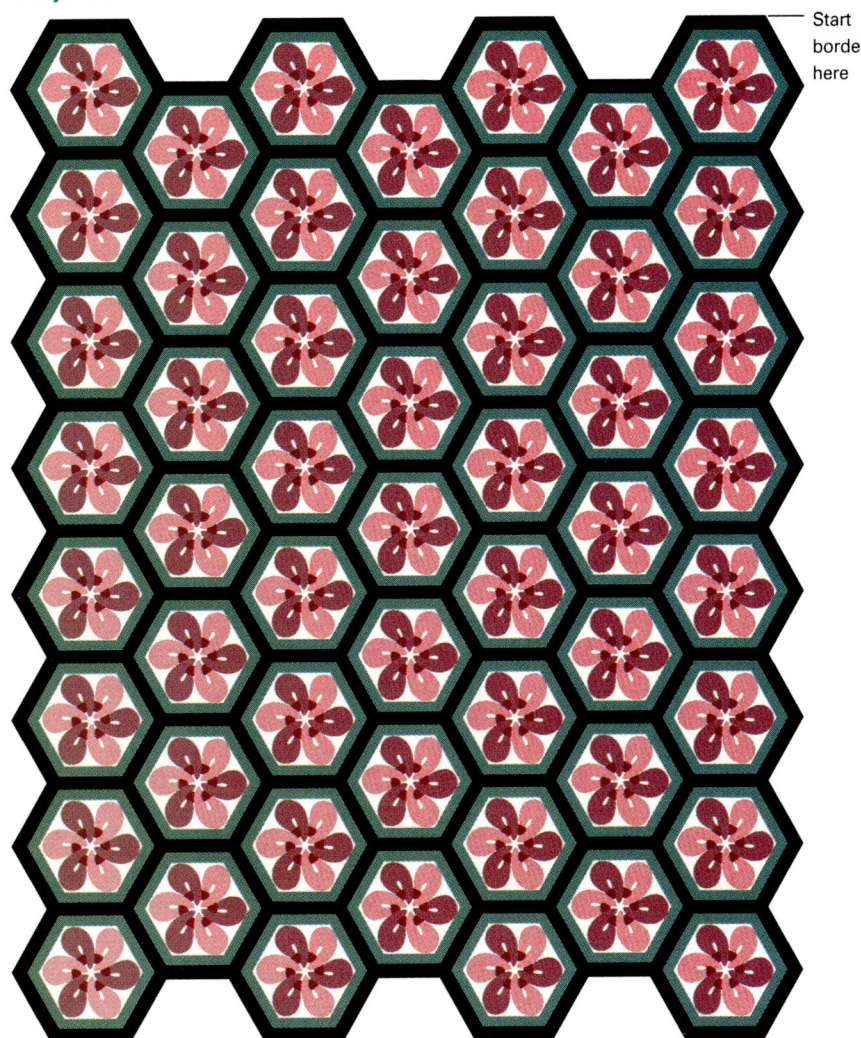

Start border here

Rainbow's End
designed by Eleanor Albano-Miles

These lively pastel colors are for brightening a country home. Made up of three panels and bordered in off-white, the bouncy puff stitches wrap you in comfort and warmth.

Size:
About 44" x 62"

Materials:
Worsted weight yarn, 25½ oz (1785 yds, 765 gms) off white; 3 oz (210 yds, 90 gms) each, yellow, peach, pink, lt purple, dk purple, blue, and green

Note: *Our photographed afghan was made with Red Heart® Classic™, Off White #3, Cornmeal #220, Lt Clay #275, Pale Rose #755, Lt Lavender #579, Lavender #584, Lt Periwinkle #827, and Lt Seafoam #683.*

Size J (6mm) crochet hook, or size required for gauge
Size 16 tapestry needle

Gauge:
3 sc = 1"

Pattern Stitch

Puff Stitch (puff st):
(YO, draw up lp in st indicated) twice; YO and draw through all 5 lps on hook—puff st made.

Instructions

Panel (make 3)

Note: *To change color at end of row, work until 2 lps of last st remain on hook. With new color, YO and draw through 2 lps on hook. Cut old color unless otherwise specified.*

With off white, ch 31.

Row 1 (right side):
Hdc in 3rd ch from hook (beg 2 skipped chs counts as an hdc) and in each rem ch, changing to yellow in last hdc—29 hdc. Ch 2 (counts as first hdc on following rows), turn.

Row 2:
Puff st (see Pattern Stitch) in each of next 27 hdc; hdc in 2nd ch of beg 2 skipped chs, changing to off white. Ch 2, turn.

Row 3:
Hdc in each st and in 2nd ch of turning ch-2, changing to peach in last hdc. Ch 2, turn.

Row 4:
Rep Row 2.

Row 5:
Rep Row 3, changing to pink.

continued

Rainbow's End

Row 6:
Rep Row 2.

Row 7:
Rep Row 3, changing to lt purple.

Row 8:
Rep Row 2.

Row 9:
Rep Row 3, changing to dk purple.

Row 10:
Rep Row 2.

Row 11:
Rep Row 3, changing to blue.

Row 12:
Rep Row 2.

Row 13:
Rep Row 3, changing to green.

Row 14:
Rep Row 2.

Row 15:
Rep Row 3, changing to yellow.

Rows 16 through 99:
Rep Rows 2 through 15 six times more.

Rows 100 through 112:
Rep Rows 2 through 14.

Row 113:
Hdc in each hdc and in 2nd ch of turning ch-2. Finish off.

Panel Border:
Hold panel with right side facing you and beg ch at top; with off white make slip knot on hook and join with an sc in first unused lp of beg ch.

Rnd 1 (right side):
2 sc in same lp as joining—corner made; working in rem unused lps of beg ch, sc in each lp to last lp; 3 sc in last lp—corner made; working along next side in ends of rows in sps formed by edge hdc and turning chs, sc in first row, 2 sc in next row; † sc in next row, 2 sc in next row †; rep from † to † to last row; sc in last row; working along Row 113, 3 sc in 2nd ch of turning ch—corner made; sc in each hdc to last hdc; 3 sc in last hdc—corner made; working along next side in ends of rows in sps formed by edge hdc and turning chs, sc in Row 113, 2 sc in next row; rep from † to † to first row; sc in first row; join in first sc.

Rnd 2:
Ch 1, sc in same sc; * corner in next sc; sc in each sc to 2nd sc of next corner; rep from * twice more; corner in next sc; sc in each sc to first sc; join in first sc.

Rnd 3:
Ch 1, sc in same sc and in next sc; * corner in next sc; sc in each sc to 2nd sc of next corner; rep from * twice more; corner in next sc; sc in each sc to first sc; join in first sc.

Rnd 4:
Ch 1, sc in same sc and in next 2 sc; * corner in next sc; sc in each sc to 2nd sc of next corner; rep from * twice more; corner in next sc; sc in each sc to first sc; join in first sc.

Rnd 5:
Ch 1, sc in same sc and in next 3 sc; * corner in next sc; sc in each sc to 2nd sc of next corner; rep from * twice more; corner in next sc; sc in each sc to first sc; join in first sc.

Rnd 6:
Ch 1, sc in same sc and in next 4 sc; * corner in next sc; sc in each sc to 2nd sc of next corner; rep from * twice more; corner in next sc; sc in each sc to first sc; join in first sc.

Finish off and weave in all ends.

Rep on rem panels.

Assembly
Hold 2 panels with wrong sides together and center colors in same direction. With tapestry needle and off white, sew together along one long edge, beginning and ending in corner ch-2 sps. Sew third panel to either panel in same manner.

Border
Hold afghan with right side facing you and one short end at top; with off white make slip knot on hook and join with an sc in 2nd sc of upper right-hand corner.

Rnd 1 (right side):
2 sc in same sc as joining—corner made; † sc in each sc to joined sc of next joining, hdc in joined sc, dc in joining, hdc in next joined sc †; rep from † to † once; sc in each sc to 2nd sc of next corner; 3 sc in 2nd sc—corner made; sc in each sc to 2nd sc of next corner; 3 sc in 2nd sc—corner made; rep from † to † twice more; sc in each sc to 2nd sc of next corner; 3 sc in 2nd sc—corner made; sc in each sc to joining sc; join in joining sc.

Rnd 2:
Ch 1, sc in same sc as joining, corner in next sc; * sc in each st to 2nd sc of next corner; corner in 2nd sc; rep from * twice more; sc in each st to first sc; join in first sc.

Finish off and weave in ends.

Strawberry Jam
designed by Eleanor Albano-Miles

What a refreshing, new look for an afghan! Each square is embellished with bright strawberries for a fresh country-style accent.

Strawberry Jam

Size:
About 48" x 60"

Materials:
Worsted weight yarn, 30 oz (2100 yds, 900 gms) off white; 16 oz (1120 yds, 480 gms) yellow; 8½ oz (595 yds, 255 gms) black; 5 oz (350 yds, 150 gms) green; 4½ oz (315 yds, 135 gms) red

Note: *Our photographed afghan was made with Red Heart® Classic™, Off White #3, Honey Gold #645, Black #12, Paddy Green #686, and Cherry Red #912.*

Size J (6mm) crochet hook, or size required for gauge
Size 16 tapestry needle

Gauge:
3 sc = 1"
4 sc rows = 1"

Pattern Stitch

Long Single Crochet (long sc):
Insert hook in sp indicated, YO and draw up lp to height of working rnd; YO and draw through 2 lps on hook—long sc made.

Instructions

Block (make 20)
With off white, ch 26.

Row 1 (right side):
Sc in 2nd ch from hook and in each rem ch—25 sc. Ch 1, turn.

Row 2:
Sc in each sc. Ch 1, turn.

Rows 3 through 28:
Rep Row 2.

Edging:

Rnd 1 (right side):
In first sc work (sc, ch 1, sc)—corner made; sc in next 23 sc, in next sc work (sc, ch 1, sc)—corner made; working along next side in ends of rows, sk Rows 28 and 27; † sc in next 9 rows, sk next row, sc in next 5 rows, sk next row, sc in next 9 rows †; sk next row, working along lower edge in unused lps of beg ch, in first lp work (sc, ch 1, sc)—corner made; sc in next 23 lps, in next lp work (sc, ch 1, sc)—corner made; working along next side in ends of rows, sk Row 1; rep from † to † once; join in first sc—100 sc. Finish off.

Hold block with right side facing you; join yellow in ch-1 sp in upper right-hand corner.

Rnd 2:
Ch 1, in same sp work (sc, ch 2, sc)—ch-2 corner made; † sc in next 25 sc, in next corner ch-1 sp work (sc, ch 2, sc)—ch-2 corner made; sc in next 25 sc †; rep from † to † once; join in first sc. Ch 1, turn.

Rnd 3:
* Sc in next 25 sc, sk next sc, in next corner ch-2 sp work ch-2 corner; sk next sc; rep from * 3 times more; join in first sc. Finish off.

Hold block with right side facing you; join black in ch-2 sp in upper right-hand corner.

Rnd 4:
Ch 1, ch-2 corner in same sp; long sc (see Pattern Stitch) in corner ch-2 sp on Rnd 2; † on working rnd, sk next sc (behind long sc), sc in next sc, long sc in next sc on Rnd 2 †; rep from † to † 11 times more; on working rnd, sc in next sc, long sc in next corner ch-2 sp on Rnd 2, sk next sc (behind long sc), on working rnd, in next ch-2 sp work ch-2 corner; long sc in same corner ch-2 sp on Rnd 2 as last long sc made; rep from † to † 12 times; on working rnd, sc in next sc, long sc in next corner ch-2 sp on Rnd 2, sk next sc (behind long sc); on working rnd, in next ch-2 sp work ch-2 corner; long sc in same corner ch-2 sp on Rnd 2 as last long sc made; rep from † to † 12 times; on working rnd, sc in next sc, long sc in next corner ch-2 sp on Rnd 2, sk next sc (behind long sc); on working rnd, in next ch-2 sp work ch-2 corner; long sc in same corner ch-2 sp on Rnd 2 as last long sc made; rep from † to † 12 times; on working rnd, sc in next sc, long sc in same corner ch-2 sp on Rnd 2 as first long sc made; join in first sc. Ch 1, turn.

Rnd 5:
Sc in same sc and in each sc to next corner ch-2 sp; ch-2 corner in next corner; * sc in each sc to next corner ch-2 sp; ch-2 corner in next corner; rep from * twice more; join in first sc. Finish off.

Hold block with right side facing you; join yellow in ch-2 sp in upper right-hand corner.

Rnd 6:
Ch 1, beg ch-2 corner in same sp; long sc in corner ch-2 sp on Rnd 4; † on working rnd, sk next sc (behind long sc), sc in next sc, long sc in next long sc on Rnd 4 †; rep from † to † 13 times more; on working rnd, sc in next sc, long sc in next corner ch-2 sp on Rnd 4, sk next sc (behind long sc); on working rnd, ch-2 corner in next corner ch-2 sp; long sc in same corner ch-2 sp on Rnd 4 as last long sc made; rep from † to † 14 times; on working rnd, sc in next sc, long sc in next corner ch-2 sp on Rnd 4, sk next sc (behind long sc); on working rnd, ch-2 corner in next corner ch-2 sp; long sc in same corner ch-2 sp on Rnd 4 as last long sc made; rep from † to † 14 times; on working rnd, sc in next sc, long sc in next corner ch-2 sp on Rnd 4 sk next sc (behind long sc); on working rnd, corner in next corner ch-2 sp; long sc in same corner ch-2 sp on Rnd 4 as last long sc made; rep from † to † 14 times; on working rnd, sc in next sc, long sc in same corner ch-2 sp on Rnd 4 as first long sc made; join in first sc. Ch 1, turn.

Rnd 7:
* Sc in next 31 sc, sk next sc, in next corner ch-2 sp work ch-2 corner; sk next sc; rep from * 3 times more; join in first sc. Finish off.

Hold block with right side facing you; join off white in ch-2 sp in upper right-hand corner.

Rnd 8:
Beg ch-2 corner in same sp; † sc in next 33 sc; ch-2 corner in next corner ch-2 sp; sc in next 33 sc †; ch-2 corner in next corner ch-2 sp; rep from † to † once; join in first sc. Finish off and weave in all ends.

Large Strawberry (make 10)
With red ch 3; join to form a ring.

Rnd 1 (right side):
Ch 1, 9 sc in ring; join in first sc.

Row 2:
Ch 1, sc in same sc and in next 4 sc—5 sc. Ch 1, turn, leaving rem sc unworked.

Row 3:
Sc in first 5 sc. Ch 1, turn.

Row 4:
2 sc in first sc; sc in next 3 sc, 2 sc in next sc—7 sc. Ch 1, turn.

Row 5:
Sc in each sc. Ch 1, turn.

Row 6:
Dec over first 2 sc (to work dec: draw up lp in each of next 2 sc, YO and draw through all 3 lps on hook—dec made); sc in next 3 sc, dec over next 2 sc—5 sc. Ch 1, turn.

Row 7:
Dec over first 2 sc; sc in next sc, dec over next 2 sc—3 sc. Finish off, leaving a 12" end for sewing.

Top:
Hold strawberry with right side facing you and Row 7 at top; join green in first sc on Row 7; long sc in next sc on Row 5; (on working rnd, sk next sc, long sc in next sc on Row 5) twice.
Finish off and weave in all ends.

Small Strawberry (make 20)
With red, ch 3; join to form a ring.

Rnd 1 (right side):
Ch 1, 7 sc in ring; join in first sc.

Row 2:
Ch 1, sc in same sc and in next 4 sc—5 sc. Ch 1, turn, leaving rem sc unworked.

continued

Strawberry Jam

Row 3:
Sc in each sc. Ch 1, turn.

Row 4:
Dec over first 2 sc; sc in next sc, dec over next 2 sc—3 sc.

Finish off, leaving a 12" end for sewing.

Top:
Hold small strawberry with right side facing you and Row 4 at top; join green in first sc on Row 4; long sc in next sc on Row 3; (on working rnd, sk next sc, long sc in next sc on Row 3) twice.

Finish off and weave in all ends.

Strawberry Seeds:
Referring to photo for placement, with tapestry needle and black, make straight stitches about 1/4" each in length, as desired.

Leaf (make 20)
With green, ch 10.

Rnd 1 (right side):
Sc in 2nd ch from hook, hdc in next ch, dc in next ch, trc in next 3 chs, dc in next ch, hdc in next ch, 3 sc in next ch; working on opposite side in unused lps of beg ch-10, hdc in next lp, dc in next lp, trc in next 3 lps, dc in next lp, hdc in next lp, sc in same ch as first sc; join in first sc.

Finish off, leaving a 12" end for sewing.

Assembly
Refer to photo for placement of strawberries, and leaves. Place pieces on right side of blocks. With tapestry needle and 12" ends, sew pieces to block. Join blocks in 5 rows of 4 blocks each. To join blocks, hold 2 blocks with right sides together and carefully matching stitches. With tapestry needle and off white, sew with overcast stitch (see Stitch Guide on page 160) through BLs only, beginning and ending in ch-2 sp of matching corners. Join blocks in rows and then sew rows together in same manner, being sure all four-corner junctions are firmly joined.

Border
Hold afghan with right side facing you; join off white in upper right-hand corner ch-2 sp; ch 1, 3 sc in same sp—corner made; * sc in each sc and in each joining to next corner ch-2 sp; 3 sc in corner ch-2 sp—corner made; rep from * twice more; sc in each sc and in each joining to first sc; join in first sc.

Finish off and weave in all ends.

Watermelon Picnic
designed by Diana Lynn Sippel

Whether you use this innovative afghan in your family room or on family outings to the park, it will set the tone for lively get togethers. This witty design is stitched in squares and the seeds are added with dabs of acrylic paint.

Watermelon Picnic

Size:
About 42" x 50"

Materials:
Worsted weight yarn, 18 oz (1260 yds, 540 gms) white; 10 oz (700 yds, 300 gms) green; 4 oz (280 yds, 120 gms) red

Note: *Our photographed afghan was made with Red Heart® Super Saver, White #311, Paddy Green #368, and Cherry Red #319.*

Size H (5mm) crochet hook, or size required for gauge
Size 16 tapestry needle
Tube of black acrylic paint (optional for seeds)

Gauge:
4 sc = 1"

Instructions

Note: *To change color, work until 2 lps of last st remain on hook. With new color, YO and draw through 2 lps on hook; cut old color unless otherwise specified.*

Motif (make 40)
With white, ch 5; join to form a ring.

Rnd 1 (right side):
Ch 4 (counts as a trc), 11 trc in ring, changing to red in last trc; 12 trc in ring, changing to white in last trc; join in 4th ch of beg ch-4—24 trc. Finish off red.

Rnd 2:
Ch 1, sc in same ch as joining; working in BLs only, * 2 sc in next trc; sc in next trc; rep from * 10 times more; sc in next trc; join in BL of first sc.

Rnd 3:
Ch 1, sc in same lp as joining; working in BLs only, (sc in next sc, 2 sc in next sc) 8 times; sc in next sc, changing to green; carry white; (2 sc in next sc, sc in next sc) 8 times; 2 sc in next sc, changing to white in last sc; join in BL only of first sc.

Rnd 4:
Ch 1, sc in same lp as joining; working in BLs only, sc in each rem sc—52 sc; join in first sc.

Rnd 5:
Ch 3 (counts as a dc), hdc in next 2 sc, sc in next 6 sc, hdc in next 2 sc, dc in next sc, in next sc work (2 dc, ch 2, 2 dc)—corner made; * dc in next sc, hdc in next 2 sc, sc in next 6 sc, hdc in next 2 sc, dc in next sc, in next sc work (2 dc, ch 2, 2 dc)—corner made; rep from * twice more, changing to green; join in 3rd ch of beg ch-3. Finish off white.

Rnd 6:
Ch 1, sc in same ch as joining and in next 13 sts, 3 sc in corner ch-2 sp; * sc in next 16 sts, 3 sc in next corner ch-2 sp; rep from * twice more; sc in next 2 sts; join in first sc.
Finish off and weave in ends.

Seeds (optional)
Referring to photo for placement, apply paint directly to watermelon sections.

Panel (make 5)

Referring to **Diagram A** for placement of watermelons, join 8 motifs for one panel. To join motifs, hold 2 motifs with right sides together, carefully matching stitches. With tapestry needle and green, sew with overcast stitch (see Stitch Guide on page 160) through BLs only across one side, beginning and ending in 2nd sc of each corner. Join remaining 6 motifs in same manner. Repeat for remaining 4 panels.

Diagram A

Panel Edgings

Panel A:

RIGHT EDGING:

Referring to **Diagram A** for direction of watermelons, hold one panel with right side facing you; with green make slip knot on hook and with join with an sc in 2nd sc in upper right-hand corner.

Row 1 (right side):
(Sc in next 18 sc and in next joining) 7 times; sc in next 17 sc, dec over next 2 sc (to work dec: draw up lp in each of next 2 sc, YO and draw through all 3 lps on hook—dec made)—152 sc. Finish off.

Note: On following rows, work over yarn not in use.

Row 2:
With white make slip knot on hook and join in BL of first sc of Row 1; working through BLs only, sc in next 3 sc, changing to red in last sc; * sc in next 4 sc, changing to white in last sc; sc in next 4 sc, changing to red in last sc; rep from * to last 4 sc; sc in last 4 sc. Finish off.

Rows 3 and 4:
Rep Row 2.

Weave in all ends. Set aside.

Panel B:

RIGHT EDGING:

Hold second panel with right side facing you and watermelons in same direction as Panel A. With green make slip knot on hook and join with an sc in 2nd sc of upper right-hand corner.

Rows 1 through 4:
Rep Rows 1 through 4 of Panel A Right Edging.

LEFT EDGING:

Hold panel with right side facing you and opposite long edge at top. With green make slip knot on hook and join with an sc in 2nd sc in upper right-hand corner; (sc in next 18 sc and in next joining) 7 times; sc in next 17 sc, dec over next 2 sc (to work dec: draw up lp in each of next 2 sc, YO and draw through all 3 lps on hook—dec made)—152 sc.

Finish off and weave in all ends. Set aside.

Panels C and D:

Work same as Panel B Right and Left Edgings.

Panel E:

LEFT EDGING:

Hold panel with right side facing you and watermelons in same direction as for Panel B Left Edging. With green make slip knot on hook and join with an sc in 2nd sc in upper right-hand corner; (sc in next 18 sc and in next joining) 7 times; sc in next 17 sc, dec over next 2 sc (to work dec: draw up lp in each of next 2 sc, YO and draw through all 3 lps on hook—dec made)—152 sc.

Finish off and weave in all ends.

Assembly

Referring to **Diagram B**, sew panels together, sewing Panel A to Panel B, Panel C to Panel B, etc. To sew panels, hold two panels with right sides together and long edge at top. With tapestry needle and green, sew with overcast stitch (see Stitch Guide on page 160) through BLs only across side. Sew remaining panels together in same manner.

Diagram B

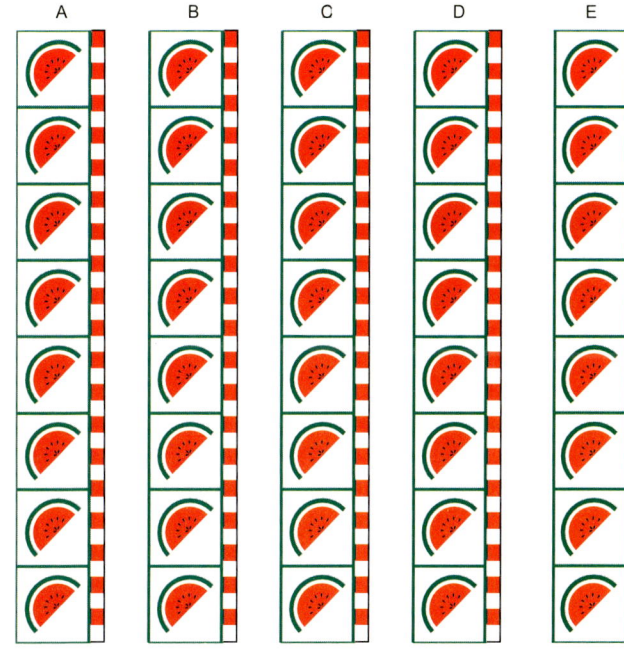

continued

Watermelon Picnic

Border

Hold afghan with right side facing you and one short end at top; with green make slip knot on hook and join with an sc in 2nd sc in upper right-hand corner.

Rnd 1 (right side):
2 sc in same sc; † sc in next 18 sc, sc in next 5 edge sc of rows †; rep from † to † 3 times more; sc in next 18 sc, 3 sc in next sc; †† sc in next 18 sc, sc in next joining ††; rep from †† to †† 6 times more, sc in next 18 sc, 3 sc in next sc; rep from † to † 4 times; sc in next 18 sc, 3 sc in next sc; rep from †† to †† 7 times; sc in next 18 sc, join in first sc.

Rnd 2:
Ch 3, 4 dc in same sp, sk next 2 sc, sl st in next sc, sk next 2 sc; * 5 dc in next sc; sk next 2 sc, sl st in next sc, sk next 2 sc; rep from * around; join in 3rd ch of beg ch-3.

Finish off and weave in all ends.

Especially for Baby

A baby will know he or she is loved when wrapped in one of these snuggy, warm afghans. As baby grows, he'll appreciate the naptime comfort of an afghan.

Angel Clouds 140
Grandma's Pride 143
Merry-Go-Rounds 146
My Little Sunshine 150
Pretty Peppermint 153
Ruffles for Baby 156

Angel Clouds

designed by Jennine Korejko

This little baby afghan reminds us of a pretty Spring day with fluffy clouds and blue skies! Crocheted in panels, this is the perfect make-ahead shower gift—just right for little boys or girls.

Size:
About 35" x 42"

Materials:
Sport weight yarn, 18 oz (1710 yds, 540 gms) blue; 11 oz (1045 yds, 330 gms) white

***Note:** Our photographed afghan was made with Caron® Simply Soft Baby Sport, Soft Blue #2504, and White #2501.*

Size F (3.75mm) crochet hook, or size required for gauge
Size 16 tapestry needle

Gauge:
8 dc = 2"
4 rows = 2"

Instructions

Panel (make 8)

Center:
With white, ch 6.

Row 1 (right side):
Dc in 4th ch from hook (beg 3 skipped chs count as a dc) and in each rem ch—4 dc. Ch 3 (counts as first dc on following rows), turn.

Row 2:
Dc in first dc; ch 1, dc in next 2 dc, ch 1, 2 dc in 3rd ch of beg 3 skipped chs—6 dc. Ch 3, turn.

Row 3:
Dc in first 2 dc; ch 1, dc in next 2 dc, ch 1, dc in next dc, 2 dc in 3rd ch of turning ch-3—8 dc. Ch 3, turn.

Row 4:
(Dc in next 2 dc, ch 1) twice; dc in next 2 dc and in 3rd ch of turning ch-3. Ch 3, turn.

Row 5:
Dec over next 2 dc [to work dec: (YO, draw up lp in next st, YO and draw through 2 lps on hook) twice; YO and draw through all 3 lps on hook—dec made]; ch 1, dc in next 2 dc, ch 1, dec over next 2 dc; dc in 3rd ch of turning ch-3—6 dc. Ch 2, turn.

Row 6:
Dc in next 3 dc, dec over next dc and 3rd ch of turning ch-3—4 dc. Ch 3, turn.

Row 7:
Dc in next 3 dc. Ch 3, turn, leaving turning ch-2 unworked.

continued

Angel Clouds

Row 8:
Dc in first dc; ch 1, dc in next 2 dc, ch 1, 2 dc in 3rd ch of turning ch-3—6 dc. Ch 3, turn.

Rows 9 through 74:
Rep Rows 3 through 8 eleven times more.

Rows 75 through 79:
Rep Rows 3 through 7. At end of Row 79, do not ch 3, do not turn.

Edging:
Working in ends of rows in sps formed by edge dc, turning chs and first dc of dec, (sl st, ch 1) twice in each row edge to beg ch; working in unused lps of beg ch, (sl st, ch 1) in each lp; working in ends of rows in sps formed by edge dc and turning chs and first dc of dec, (sl st, ch 1) twice in each row edge; working in unworked dc on Row 79, (sl st, ch 1) in each dc; join in first sl st.

Finish off and weave in ends.

Border
Hold one panel with right side facing you and Row 79 to right. Working behind edging, join blue around post (see Stitch Guide on page 160) of 3rd dc on Row 79.

Rnd 1:
Ch 3 (counts as a dc), 3 dc around same post as joining; working behind edging in ends of rows, † 3 dc around next dc; 3 hdc around first dc of next dec; 3 sc around next dc; 3 hdc around next dc; 3 dc around next dc; 2 dc around next dc †; rep from † to † 11 times more; †† 3 dc around next dc; 3 hdc around first dc of next dec; 3 sc around next dc; 3 hdc around next dc; 3 dc around first dc of next dec ††; 4 dc around next dc; ch 2; working along opposite side of panel, 4 dc around next dc; rep from † to † 12 times; rep from †† to †† once; 4 dc around next dc, ch 2; join in 3rd ch of beg ch-3.

Rnd 2:
Ch 3, dc in next 18 sts; † sk next 2 dc, (dc in next 15 sts, sk next 2 dc) 11 times; dc in next 19 sts, ch 2, 3 dc in next ch-2 sp; ch 2 †; dc in next 19 sts; rep from † to † once; join in 3rd ch of beg ch-3.

Rnd 3:
Ch 2; † dc in next 14 dc, trc in next 2 dc, sk next 4 dc, trc in next 2 dc, (dc in next 7 dc, trc in next 2 dc, sk next 4 dc, trc in next 2 dc) 11 times; dc in next 14 dc, hdc in next dc, 3 sc in next ch-2 sp; sc in next 3 dc, 3 sc in next ch-2 sp †; hdc in next dc; rep from † to † once; join in 2nd ch of beg ch-2.

Finish off and weave in ends.

Assembly
Hold two panels with wrong sides together. With tapestry needle and blue, sew panels with overcast stitch (see Stitch Guide on page 160) through BLs only, beginning and ending about 2" from ends. Sew remaining panels together in same manner.

Grandma's Pride
designed by Jennine Korejko

That irresistible baby will feel the love when wrapped in this colorful afghan. Bright pastel granny squares are all crocheted first, then are joined together as their pretty scalloped white edging is added.

Grandma's Pride

Size:
About 32" x 40"

Materials:
Sport weight yarn, 5½ oz (522 yds, 165 gms) pink; 12 oz (1140 yds, 360 gms) white; 1½ oz (142 yds, 45 gms) each, green, blue, and lavender

Note: Our photographed model was made with Patons Look At Me!, White #6351, Lavender #6358, and Mint Green #6361; Patons Astra, Pink #2845 and Blue #2774.

Size F (3.75mm) crochet hook, or size required for gauge
Size 16 tapestry needle

Gauge:
9 dc = 2"
one square = 6" x 6"

Instructions

Squares

Square A (make 12):
With pink, ch 4; join to form a ring.

Rnd 1 (right side):
Ch 1, (3 sc in ring, ch 2) 4 times; join in first sc—12 sc. Finish off.

Rnd 2:
With wrong side facing you, join white in any ch-2 sp, ch 1, in same sp work (sc, ch 2, sc)—corner made; trc in next sc, sc in next sc, trc in next sc; * in next ch-2 sp work (sc, ch 2, sc)—corner made; trc in next sc, sc in next sc, trc in next sc; rep from * twice more; join in first sc. Finish off.

Rnd 3:
With right side facing you, join pink in any corner ch-2 sp, ch 1, in same sp work corner; * sc in next 5 sts, in next ch-2 sp work corner; rep from * twice more; sc in next 5 sts; join in first sc—28 sc. Finish off.

Rnd 4:
With wrong side facing you, join blue in any corner ch-2 sp, ch 1, corner in same sp; trc in next sc, (sc in next sc, trc in next sc) 3 times; * corner in next ch-2 sp; trc in next sc, (sc in next sc, trc in next sc) 3 times; rep from * twice more; join in first sc. Finish off.

Rnd 5:
With right side facing you, join pink in any corner ch-2 sp, ch 1, corner in same sp; sc in next 9 sts; * corner in next ch-2 sp; sc in next 9 sc; rep from * twice more; join in first sc—44 sc. Finish off.

Rnd 6:
With wrong side facing you, join purple in any corner ch-2 sp, ch 1, corner in same sp; trc in next sc, (sc in next sc, trc in next sc) 5 times; * corner in next ch-2 sp; trc in next sc, (sc in next sc, trc in next sc) 5 times; rep from * twice more; join in first sc. Finish off.

Rnd 7:
With right side facing you, join pink in any corner ch-2 sp, corner in same sp; sc in next 13 sts; corner in next corner; sc in next 13 sts; rep from * twice more; join in first sc—60 sc.

Finish off and weave in all ends.

Square B (make 12):
Work same as Square A, using purple on Rnd 2, green on Rnd 4, white on Rnd 6.

Square C (make 9):
Work same as Square A, using white on Rnd 2, blue on Rnd 4, purple on Rnd 6.

Square D (make 9):
Work same as Square A, using blue on Rnd 2, white on Rnd 4, green on Rnd 6.

Assembly

Join squares in 7 rows of 6 squares each. To join squares, with white, work 3 additional rnds on each square joining in last rnd. Begin by working First Square; work Second Square joining to First Square on Rnd 3.

First Square:

Hold one Square A with right side facing you; join white in any corner ch-2 sp.

Rnd 1:
Ch 1, in same sp work (sc, ch 3, sc); * † ch 3, sk next sc, sc in next sc, ch 3, (sk next 2 sc, sc in next sc, ch 3) 4 times; sk next sc †; in next corner ch-2 sp work (sc, ch 3, sc); rep from * twice more, then rep from † to † once; join in first sc—28 ch-3 sps.

Rnd 2:
Ch 1, sc in same sc; 3 sc in next ch-3 sp; * † sc in next sc, (2 sc in next ch-3 sp, sc in next sc) 5 times †; sc in next sc, 2 sc in next ch-3 sp; 3 sc in next ch-3 sp; rep from * twice more; join in first sc—88 sc.

Rnd 3:
Ch 1, sc in same sc; sk next sc; * in next sc work (3 dc, ch 1, 3 dc)—shell made; sk next sc, sc in next sc, [sk next 2 sc, in next sc work (3 dc, ch 1, 3 dc)—shell made; sk next 2 sc, sc in next sc] 3 times; sk next sc, in next sc work (3 dc, ch 1, 3 dc)—shell made; sk next sc; rep from * twice more; [sc in next sc, sk next 2 sc, in next sc work (3 dc, ch 1, 3 dc)—shell made; sk next 2 sc] 3 times; join in first sc. Finish off.

Second Square:

Hold one Square B with right side facing you; join white in any corner ch-2 sp.

Rnds 1 and 2:
Rep Rnds 1 and 2 of First Square.

Rnd 3 (joining rnd):
Ch 1, sc in same sc; sk next sc, shell in next sc; sk next sc, sc in next sc, (sk next 2 sc, shell in next sc, sk next 2 sc, sc in next sc) 3 times; sk next sc, 3 dc in next sc; hold completed square and working square with wrong sides tog; on completed square, sc in ch-1 sp of corner shell; on working square, 3 dc in same sc; sk next sc, sc in next sc; † sk next 2 sc, 3 dc in next sc; on completed square, sc in ch-1 sp of next shell; on working square, 3 dc in same sc; sk next 2 sc, sc in next sc †; rep from † to † twice more; sk next sc, 3 dc in next sc; on completed square, sc in ch-1 sp of next corner shell; on working square, 3 dc in same sc; sk next sc, sc in next sc, (sk next 2 sc, shell in next sc, sk next 2 sc, sc in next sc) 3 times; sk next sc, shell in next sc; sk next sc, (sc in next sc, sk next 2 sc, shell in next sc, sk next 2 sc) 3 times; join in first sc. Finish off.

Referring to **Layout** for color placement, join remaining squares in same manner, working joinings in similiar manner and being sure all four-corner junctions are firmly joined.

Weave in all ends.

Layout

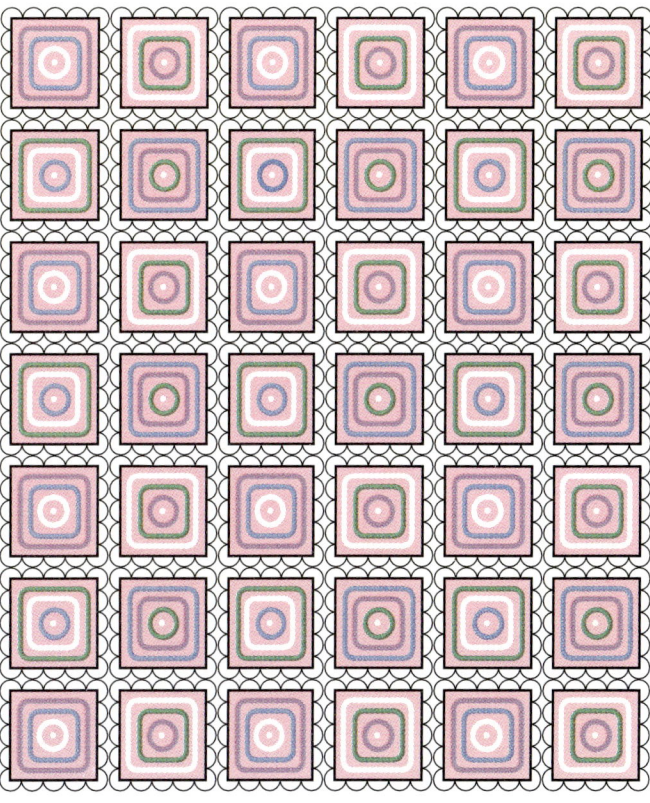

145

Merry-Go-Rounds *designed by Nanette Seale*

Lacy crocheted motifs will put the whole family in a merry mood. Using pastel colors in baby weight yarn makes this the perfect warm weather wrap for baby.

Size:
About 34" x 44"

Materials:
Baby weight yarn, 8 oz (1360 yds, 240 gms) white; 4 oz (680 yds, 120 gms) each, pink and blue; 3½ oz (595 yds, 105 gms) each, yellow and lavender

Note: Our photographed afghan was made with Red Heart® Baby Pompadour, White #1, Light Pink #722, Baby Blue #802, Baby Yellow #224, and Lilac #571.

Size E (3.5mm) crochet hook, or size required for gauge
Size 16 tapestry needle

Gauge:
11 dc = 2"
one large motif = 7" in diameter

Pattern Stitches

Beginning Cluster (beg CL):
Ch 3, keeping last lp of each dc on hook, 2 dc in sp indicated; YO and draw through all 3 lps on hook—beg CL made.

Cluster (CL):
Keeping last lp of each dc on hook, 3 dc in st or sp indicated; YO and draw through all 4 lps on hook—CL made.

Instructions

Center
Center of afghan is worked in motifs. Refer to **Layout** on page 148 for color and placement of motifs. Begin center by working Motif A. Work Motif B joining it to Motif A. Work remainder of center in same manner.

Motif A
Ch 3, join to form a ring.

Rnd 1 (right side):
Ch 3 (counts as a dc on this and following rnds), 15 dc in ring; join in 3rd ch of beg ch-3—16 dc.

Rnd 2:
Ch 4 (counts as a dc and a ch-1 sp on this and following rnds); * dc in next dc, ch 1; rep from * 14 times more; join in 3rd ch of beg ch-4.

Rnd 3:
Sl st in next ch-1 sp, in same sp work beg CL (see Pattern Stitches); ch 2, in next ch-1 sp work CL (see Pattern Stitches); ch 2; * in next ch-1 sp work CL; ch 2; rep from * 13 times more; join in top of beg CL—16 CLs.

continued

Merry-Go-Rounds

Layout

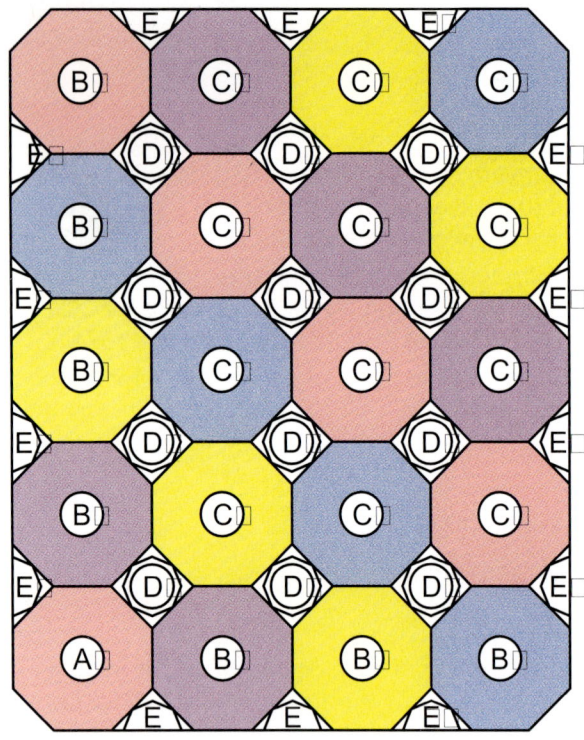

Rnd 4:
Ch 4, dc in same sp—beg V-st made; ch 3; * in top of next CL work (dc, ch 1, dc)—V-st made; ch 3; rep from * 14 times more; join in 3rd ch of beg ch-4.

Rnd 5:
Sl st in next ch, in next dc, and in next ch-3 sp; ch 3, 9 dc in same sp; ch 3, sk next ch-3 sp; * 10 dc in next ch-3 sp; ch 3, sk next ch-3 sp; rep from * 6 times more; join in 3rd ch of beg ch-3.

Rnd 6:
Ch 4; * † (dc in next dc, ch 1) 8 times; dc in next dc, sc in next ch-3 sp †; dc in next dc, ch 1; rep from * 6 times more, then rep from † to † once; join in 3rd ch of beg ch-4.

Rnd 7:
Sl st in next ch-1 sp, ch 1, sc in same sp; * † ch 3, sk next ch-1 sp, CL in next ch-1 sp; ch 3, sk next ch-1 sp, in next ch-1 sp work (CL, ch 3) twice; sk next ch-1 sp, CL in next ch-1 sp; ch 3, sk next ch-1 sp, sc in next ch-1 sp, ch 1 †; sc in next ch-1 sp; rep from * 6 times more, then rep from † to † once; join in first sc.

Rnd 8:
Sl st in next 3 chs and in next CL; beg V-st in same CL; ch 3, V-st in next CL; * † in next ch-3 sp work (2 dc, ch 3, 2 dc)—shell made; V-st in next CL; ch 3 †; V-st in each of next 2 CLs; ch 3, V-st in next CL; rep from * 6 times more, then rep from † to † once; V-st in next CL; join in 3rd ch of beg ch-4. Finish off.

Motif B
Work same as Motif A through Rnd 7.

Rnd 8 (one-sided joining):
Sl st in next 3 chs and in next CL; work beg V-st in same CL; ch 3; * V-st in next CL; shell in next ch-3 sp; V-st in next CL; ch 3, V-st in each of next 2 CLs; ch 3; rep from * 5 times more; V-st in next CL; 2 dc in next ch-3 sp; ch 1; hold wrong side of completed motif facing wrong side of working motif and carefully match sts; on completed motif, sl st in ch-3 sp of corresponding shell, ch 1; on working motif, 2 dc in same ch-3 sp; V-st in next CL; ch 3, dc in next CL; on completed motif, sl st in next V-st; on working motif, dc in same CL and in next CL; on completed motif, sl st in ch-1 sp of next V-st; on working motif, dc in same CL, ch 3, V-st in next CL; 2 dc in next ch-3 sp; ch 1; on completed motif, sl st in ch-3 sp of next shell; on working motif, 2 dc in same sp; V-st in next CL; ch 3, V-st in next CL; join in 3rd ch of beg ch-4. Finish off.

Motif C
Work same as Motif A through Rnd 7.

Rnd 8 (two-sided joining):
Sl st in next 3 chs and in next CL; work beg V-st; ch 3; * V-st in next CL; shell in next ch-3 sp; V-st in next CL; ch 3, V-st in each of next 2 CLs; ch 3; rep from * 3 times more; † V-st in next CL; 2 dc in next ch-3 sp; ch 1; hold wrong side of completed motif facing wrong side of working motif and carefully matching sts; on completed motif, sl st in ch-3 sp of corresponding shell; ch 1; on working motif, 2 dc in same ch-3 sp; V-st in next CL; ch 3, dc in next CL; on completed motif, sl st in ch-1 sp of next V-st; on working motif, dc in same CL, and in next CL; on completed motif, sl st in V-st; on working motif, dc in same CL, ch 3, V-st in next CL; 2 dc in next ch-3 sp; ch 1; on completed motif, sl st in ch-3 sp of next shell; on working motif, 2 dc in same sp; V-st in next CL; ch 3, V-st in next CL; join in 3rd ch of beg ch-4. Finish off.

Motif D
Note: Motif D will fill in center sp of 4 joined motifs and will be joined to each of the 4 motifs.

With white, work same as Motif A through Rnd 3.

Rnd 4 (joining rnd):
Beg V-st in same sp as joining; ch 3, dc in next CL; hold wrong side of one completed motif facing wrong side of working motif; sl st in joined ch-3 sp on completed motif; * † on working motif, dc in same CL, ch 3, V-st in next CL; ch 3, dc in next CL; on completed motif, sk next V-st and next ch-3 sp, sl st in sp between next 2 V-sts; on working motif, dc in same CL, ch 3, V-st in next CL; ch 3 †; dc in next CL; on next completed motif, sl st in joined ch-3 sp; rep from * twice more, then rep from † to † once; join in 3rd ch of beg ch-4.

Finish off and weave in ends.

Rep Motif D between remaining joined motifs.

Motif E

Note: Motif E will fill in sp on edge of 2 motifs and will be joined to both motifs.

With white, ch 3; join to form a ring.

Row 1 (right side):
Ch 3 (counts as a dc), 9 dc in ring—10 dc. Ch 4 (counts as first dc and ch-1 sp on following rows), turn.

Row 2:
(Dc in next dc, ch 1) 8 times; dc in 3rd ch of beg ch-3. Turn.

Row 3:
Sl st in first ch-1 sp, beg CL in same sp; ch 2, (CL in next sp, ch 2) 7 times; CL in sp formed by turning ch-4. Ch 3, turn.

Row 4:
Hold wrong side of completed motif facing right side of working motif; on completed motif, sl st in ch-3 sp of first shell to right of first joined ch-3 sp; on working motif, dc in first CL; † ch 3, V-st in top of next CL, ch 3, dc in top of next CL †; on completed motif, sk next 2 dc, next V-st, and next ch-3 sp; sl st between next 2 V-sts; on working motif, dc in same CL; rep from † to † once; on next completed motif, sl st in next joined ch-3 sp, on working motif dc in same CL; rep from † to † once; on completed motif, sk next 2 dc, next V-st, and next ch-3 sp; sl st between next 2 V-sts; on working motif, dc in same CL; rep from † to † once; on next completed motif, sl st in next ch-3 sp; on working motif, dc in same CL. Finish off.

Edging

Hold afghan with right side facing you and one short end at top; join white in unused ch-3 sp of 2nd shell in upper right-hand corner.

Rnd 1:
Ch 5; † dc in next dc, ch 2, sk next dc, (dc in next dc, ch 2) 8 times; sk next dc, dc in next dc, ch 2, dc in next ch-3 sp; †† working along edge of Motif E, dc in side of next dc, in next CL, in side of next 2 dc, in base of same dc, in ring, in base of next dc, in side of next 2 dc, in next CL, and in side of next dc; working along next motif, dc in next ch-3 sp, ch 2 †; rep from † to † twice more; †† dc in next dc, ch 2, sk next dc, (dc in next dc, ch 2) 8 times; sk next dc, dc in next dc, ch 2, dc in next ch-3 sp ††; rep from †† to †† once more; rep from † to † 4 times; rep from †† to †† twice; rep from † to † 3 times; rep from †† to †† twice; rep from † to † 4 times; rep from †† to †† once; dc in next dc, ch 2, sk next dc, (dc in next dc, ch 2) 8 times; sk next dc, dc in next dc, ch 2; join in 3rd ch of beg ch-5.

Rnd 2:
Ch 1, sc in same ch as joining; ch 2, dc in next dc, ch 2; * sc in next dc, ch 2, dc in next dc, ch 2; rep from * around; join in first sc.

Rnd 3:
Sl st in next 2 chs and in next dc, ch 8 (counts as a dc and a ch-5 sp on this and following rnds), sk next sc; * dc in next dc, ch 5, sk next sc; rep from * around; join in 3rd ch of beg ch-8.

Rnd 4:
Ch 5 (counts as a dc and a ch-2 sp), sc in next ch-5 sp, ch 2; * dc in next dc, ch 2, sc in next ch-5 sp, ch 2; rep from * around; join in 3rd ch of beg ch-5.

Rnd 5:
Ch 8, sk next sc; * dc in next dc, ch 5, sk next sc; rep from * around; join in 3rd ch of beg ch-8.

Rnds 6 and 7:
Rep Rnds 4 and 5.

Rnd 8:
Rep Rnd 4.

Rnd 9:
Beg V-st; (ch 5, sk next sc, dc in next dc) 4 times; * ch 5, sk next sc, V-st in next dc; (ch 5, sk next sc, dc in next dc) 4 times; rep from * around; ch 5; join in 3rd ch of beg ch-4. Finish off.

Rnd 10:
Join pink in 2nd dc of beg V-st, beg CL in same sp; (ch 3, sc in next ch-5 sp, ch 3, CL in next dc) 5 times; * ch 3, CL in next dc; (ch 3, sc in next ch-5 sp, ch 3, CL in next dc) 5 times; rep from * around; ch 3; join in top of first CL. Finish off.

Rnd 11:
Join blue in top of beg CL, beg CL in same sp; ch 3; * † (sc in next ch-3 sp, ch 3) twice; CL in next CL; ch 3 †; rep from † to † 4 times more; sc in next ch-3 sp, ch 3, CL in next CL; rep from * 39 times more, then rep from † to † 4 times; (sc in next ch-3 sp, ch 3) twice; join in top of beg CL.

Finish off and weave in all ends.

My Little Sunshine
designed by Jennine Korejko

You won't be able to stop smiling as your precious little one peeks out from under this bright, happy afghan. This clever design is crocheted in squares making it an ideal project to take along and work on away from home.

Size:
About 32" x 32"

Materials:
Sport weight yarn, 11 oz (1045 yds, 330 gms) yellow; 4 oz (380 yds, 120 gms) white; 2 oz (190 yds, 60 gms) each, blue and green; 1½ oz (142 yds, 45 gms) each, pink and lavender

Note: *Our photographed afghan was made with Patons Astra, Baby Yellow #2759, White #2751, Medium Blue #2774, Mint #2212, Baby Pink #2752, and Lavender #2724.*

Size F (3.75mm) crochet hook, or size required for gauge
Size 16 tapestry needle

Gauge:
9 dc = 2"
one square = 4" x 4"

Pattern Stitches

Front Post Triple Crochet (FPtrc):
YO twice, draw up lp in st indicated, (YO, draw through 2 lps on hook) 3 times—FPtrc made.

Front Post Double Crochet (FPdc):
YO, draw up lp in st indicated, (YO, draw through 2 lps on hook) twice—FPdc made.

Instructions

Square A (make 12)
With pink, ch 4; join to form a ring.

Rnd 1 (right side):
Ch 5 (counts as a dc and a ch-2 sp), (dc in ring, ch 2) 7 times; join in 3rd ch of beg ch-5—8 ch-2 sps. Finish off.

Rnd 2:
Join blue in any ch-2 sp; ch 3 (counts as a dc on this and following rnds), 2 dc in same sp; 3 dc in next ch-2 sp; ch 3; * 3 dc in each of next 2 ch-2 sps, ch 3; rep from * twice more; join in 3rd ch of beg ch-3—24 dc. Finish off.

Rnd 3:
Join yellow in any ch-3 sp, ch 1, 3 sc in same sp—corner made; * sc in next 6 dc, 3 sc in next ch-3 sp—corner made; rep from * twice more; sc in next 6 dc; join in first sc—36 sc. Change to green by drawing lp through; cut yellow.

continued

My Little Sunshine

Rnd 4:
Ch 3, 3 dc in next sc—dc corner made; * dc in next 8 sc, 3 dc in next sc—dc corner made; rep from * twice more; dc in next 7 sc; join in 3rd ch of beg ch-3—44 dc. Change to yellow by drawing lp through; cut green.

Rnd 5:
Ch 1, sc in same ch as joining; *† FPtrc (see Pattern Stitches on page 151) around first corner sc on Rnd 3; sk next dc, sc in next dc, FPtrc around next corner sc on Rnd 3; sc in same dc as last sc made, FPtrc around next corner sc on Rnd 3; sk next dc †; sc in next 8 dc; rep from * twice more, then rep from † to † once; sc in next 7 dc; join in first sc.

Rnd 6:
Ch 1, sc in same sc and in next 2 sts, 3 hdc in next FPtrc; (sc in next 12 sts, 3 hdc in next FPtrc) 3 times; sc in next 9 sts; join in first sc. Finish off.

Square B (make 13)
Work same as Square A using white on Rnd 1, lavender on Rnd 2, and pink on Rnd 4.

Square C (make 14)
Work same as Square A using blue on Rnd 1, green on Rnd 2, and white on Rnd 4.

Square D (make 13)
Work same as Square A using lavender on Rnd 1, pink on Rnd 2, and blue on Rnd 4.

Square E (make 12)
Work same as Square A using green on Rnd 1, white on Rnd 2, and lavender on Rnd 4.

Assembly
Referring to **Layout** for color placement, join squares in 8 rows of 8 squares each. To join squares, hold two squares with wrong sides together. With tapestry needle and yellow, sew with overcast stitch (see Stitch Guide on page 160) along one side, beginning and ending in center hdc of each corner. Join squares in rows; then join rows together in same manner, being sure all four-corner junctions are firmly joined.

Edging
Hold afghan with right side facing you; join yellow in 2nd hdc in upper right-hand corner.

Rnd 1:
Ch 4 (counts as a dc and a ch-1 sp), in same hdc work (dc, ch 1) 3 times—corner made; * sk next hdc, (dc in next sc, ch 1, sk next sc) 6 times; dc in next hdc, ch 1; † dc in joining, ch 1, sk next hdc, dc in next hdc, (ch 1, sk next sc, dc in next sc) 6 times; ch 1 †; rep from † to † 6 times more; sk next hdc, in next corner hdc work (dc, ch 1) 4 times—corner made; rep from * 3 times more; join in 3rd ch of beg ch-4.

Rnd 2:
Ch 3 (counts as a dc on this and following rnds), dc in next ch-1 sp and in next dc, in next ch-1 sp work (dc, ch 3, dc)—dc corner made; * dc in each dc and in each ch-1 sp to next corner ch-1 sp; in corner ch-1 sp work (dc, ch 3, dc)—dc corner made; rep from * twice more; dc in each dc and in each ch-1 sp to beg ch-3; join in 3rd ch of beg ch-3.

Rnd 3:
Ch 1, FPdc (see Pattern Stitches on page 151) around beg ch on 2nd rnd below; sc in next dc, FPdc around next dc on 2nd rnd below; sc in next dc, in next corner ch-3 sp work (sc, ch 3, sc)—sc corner made; sc in next dc; *† FPdc around next dc on 2nd rnd below; sc in next dc †; rep from † to † to next corner; in corner ch-3 sp work (sc, ch 3, sc)—sc corner made; sc in next dc; rep from * twice more; sc in next dc; rep from † to † to first FPdc; join in BL of first FPdc.

Rnd 4:
Ch 3, working in BLs only, sk next st, sl st in next st, ch 3, sk next st, sl st in next st, ch 3, sl st in corner ch-3 sp, ch 3; * sl st in next sc, ch 3; † sk next sc, sl st in next st, ch 3 †; rep from † to † to next corner; sl st in corner ch-3 sp, ch 3; rep from * twice more; sl st in next sc, ch 3; rep from † to † to joining sl st; join in joining sl st.

Finish off and weave in all ends.

Layout

Pretty Peppermint
designed by Jennine Korejko

This afghan is quick to make when you're short on time and need a baby gift in a hurry. Pretty pink and white striped panels are edged in scallops and joined for a feminine look—but change pink to another color and it won't be just for little girls.

Pretty Peppermint

Size:
About 32" x 40"

Materials:
Sport weight yarn, 10 oz (950 yds, 300 gms) each, pink and white

Note: *Our photographed afghan was made with Lion Brand® Baby Soft®, Pastel Pink #101 and White #100.*

Size G (4.25mm) crochet hook, or size required for gauge
Size 16 tapestry needle

Gauge:
4 dc = 1"

Pattern Stitch

Cluster (CL):
Keeping last lp of each dc on hook, 2 dc in st indicated; YO and draw through all 3 lps on hook—CL made.

Instructions

Panel (make 7)

Center:
With pink, ch 15.

Row 1 (right side):
In 4th ch from hook (beg 3 skipped chs count as a dc) work [CL (see Pattern Stitch), ch 2, CL]; * sk next 2 chs, in next ch work (CL, ch 2, CL); rep from * twice more; sk next ch, dc in next ch. Ch 1, turn.

Row 2:
Sc in first dc, 3 sc in each of next 4 ch-2 sps; sc in 3rd ch of beg 3 skipped chs—14 sc. Ch 1, turn.

Row 3:
Sc in first sc, ch 2, dec over next 3 sc (to work dec: draw up lp in next sc, sk next sc, draw up lp in next sc, YO and draw through all 3 lps on hook—dec made); ch 2; * dec over next 3 sc, ch 2; rep from * twice more; sc in next sc—5 ch-2 sps. Finish off.

Hold piece with right side facing you; join white in first sc of Row 3.

Row 4:
Ch 3 (counts as a dc on this and following rows), * 2 dc in next ch-2 sp, dc in next st; rep from * 4 times more—16 dc. Finish off.

Hold piece with right side facing you; join pink in 3rd ch of beg ch-3 of Row 4.

Row 5:
Ch 3, sk next 2 dc; * in next dc work (CL, ch 2, CL); sk next 2 dc; rep from * 3 times more; dc in next dc—4 ch-2 sps. Ch 1, turn.

Row 6:
Sc in first dc, 3 sc in each of next 4 ch-2 sps; sc in 3rd ch of beg ch-3. Ch 1, turn.

Row 7:
Sc in first sc, ch 2, dec over next 3 sc; ch 2; * dec over next 3 sc, ch 2; rep from * twice more; sc in next sc—5 ch-2 sps. Finish off.

Hold piece with right side facing you; join white in first sc of prev Row 7.

Row 8:
Ch 1, sc in same sc as joining; * 2 sc in next ch-2 sp, sc in next st; rep from * 4 times more—16 sc. Finish off.

Hold piece with right side facing you; join pink in first sc of Row 8.

Row 9:
Ch 3, sk next 2 sc; * in next sc work (CL, ch 2, CL); sk next 2 sc; rep from * 3 times more; dc in next sc—4 ch-2 sps. Ch 1, turn.

Rows 10 through 105:
Rep Rows 2 through 9 eleven times more.

Rows 106 through 110:
Rep Rows 2 through 6.

Row 111:
Sc in each sc.
Finish off and weave in all ends.

Edging:
Hold center with right side facing you; join white in first sc in upper right-hand corner.

Rnd 1 (right side):
Ch 3 (counts as dc), 2 dc in same sc as joining—beg corner made; working across Row 111, dc in next 12 sc, 3 dc in next sc—corner made; working along next side in ends of sc rows and in sps formed by edge dc and turning chs, dc in Row 110, 2 dc in each of next 2 rows; dc in next 2 rows; * 2 dc in next row; dc in next 3 rows, 2 dc in each of next 2 rows; dc in next 2 rows; rep from * 12 times more; 2 dc in Row 1; working in unused lps of beg ch and in sps formed by skipped chs, 3 dc in first unused lp—corner made; dc in next sp, dc in next unused lp, (2 dc in next sp, dc in next unused lp) 3 times; dc in next sp, 3 dc in next unused lp—corner made; working along next side in ends of sc rows and in sps formed by edge dc and turning chs, 2 dc in Row 1; ** † dc in next 2 rows, 2 dc in each of next 2 rows †; dc in next 3 rows, 2 dc in next row; rep from ** 12 times more, then rep from † to † once; dc in next row; join in 3rd ch of beg ch-3.

Rnd 2:
Sl st in next dc, ch 1, in same dc work (3 sc, ch 2, 3 sc)—corner made; † sk next 2 dc, in next dc work (2 sc, ch 2, 2 sc) †; rep from † to † 3 times more; sk next 2 dc, in next dc work (3 sc, ch 2, 3 sc)—corner made; rep from † to † 51 times; sk next 3 dc, in next dc work (3 sc, ch 2, 3 sc)—corner made; rep from † to † 4 times; sk next 2 dc, in next dc work (3 sc, ch 2, 3 sc)—corner made; rep from † to † 49 times; sk next 3 dc, in next dc work (2 sc, ch 2, 2 sc); rep from † to † 51 times; sk next 3 sts; join in first sc—114 ch-2 sps. Finish off.

Assembly

First Panel:
Hold one panel with right side facing you and one short end at top; with pink make slip knot on hook and join with an sc in upper right-hand corner ch-2 sp, 2 sc in same sp—corner made; † sl st in next 5 sc, in next ch-2 sp work (sc, ch 1, sc); †† sl st in next 4 sc, in next ch-2 sp work (sc, ch 1, sc) ††; rep from †† to †† twice more; sl st in next 5 sc, 3 sc in next corner ch-2 sp—corner made; sl st in next 5 sc, in next ch-2 sp work (sc, ch 1, sc); rep from †† to †† 51 times; sl st in next 5 sc †; 3 sc in next corner ch-2 sp—corner made; rep from † to † once; join in joining sc. Finish off.

Second Panel:
Hold one panel with right side facing you and one short end at top; with pink make slip knot on hook and join with an sc in upper right-hand corner ch-2 sp, 2 sc in same sp—corner made; sl st in next 5 sc, in next ch-2 sp work (sc, ch 1, sc); † sl st in next 4 sc, in next ch-2 sp work (sc, ch 1, sc) †; rep from † to † twice more; sl st in next 5 sc, 3 sc in next corner ch-2 sp—corner made; sl st in next 5 sc, in next ch-2 sp work (sc, ch 1, sc); rep from † to † 51 times; sl st in next 5 sc, 3 sc in next corner ch-2 sp—corner made; sl st in next 5 sc, in next ch-2 sp work (sc, ch 1, sc); †† sl st in next 4 sc, in next ch-2 sp work (sc, ch 1, sc) ††; rep from †† to †† twice more; sl st in next 5 sc, 3 sc in next corner ch-2 sp—corner made; sl st in next 5 sc, sc in next ch-2 sp; hold working panel with wrong side facing prev panel with centers facing same direction; sc in corresponding ch-1 sp of prev panel; on working panel, sc in same ch-2 sp; * sl st in next 4 sc, sc in next ch-1 sp; on prev panel, sc in next ch-2 sp; on working panel, sc in same ch-2 sp; rep from * 51 times more; sl st in next 5 sts; join in joining sc. Finish off.

Third through Seventh Panels:
Work same as for Second Panel.

Weave in all ends.

Ruffles for Baby
designed by Mary Ann Frits

Wrap your precious little one in a luscious layer of ruffles. First the mint green background is crocheted and then every sixth row is embellished with a row of white ruffles.

Size:
About 30" x 38"

Materials:
Sport weight yarn, 17 oz (1564 yds, 476 gms) lt green; 14 oz (1288 yds, 392 gms) white

Note: *Our photographed afghan was made with Lion Brand® Baby Soft, Pastel Green #156 and White #100.*

Size F (3.75mm) crochet hook, or size required for gauge
Size 16 tapestry needle

Gauge:
9 sc = 2"

Instructions

Center
With lt green, ch 226.

Row 1 (right side):
Sc in 2nd ch from hook and in next 6 chs; * 3 sc in next ch; sc in next 6 chs, sk next 2 chs, sc in next 6 chs; rep from * 13 times more; 3 sc in next ch; sc in next 7 chs. Ch 1, turn.

Row 2:
Sk first sc, sc in next 7 sc; * 3 sc in next sc; sc in next 6 sc, sk next 2 sc, sc in next 6 sc; rep from * 13 times more; 3 sc in next sc; sc in next 6 sc, sk next sc, sc in next sc. Ch 1, turn.

Row 3:
Working in BLs only, rep Row 2.

Rows 4 through 6:
Rep Row 2.

Rep Rows 3 through 6 until piece measures about 38". At end of last row, do not ch 1.

Finish off and weave in all ends.

Lace Rows
Hold afghan with right side facing you and and last row worked at top; with white make slip knot on hook and join with an sc in first unused lp of Row 2; ch 3, sl st in 3rd ch from hook, in each rem unused lp work (sc, ch 3, sl st in 3rd ch from hook). Finish off.

Repeat on each row of unused lps.

Weave in all ends.

General Information

Abbreviations and Symbols

beg	begin(ning)
BL(s)	back loop(s)
ch(s)	chain(s)
CL(s)	cluster(s)
dc	double crochet(s)
dec	decrease(-ing)
dtrc	double triple crochet(s)
FPdc	front post double crochet(s)
FPhdc	front post half double crochet(s)
FPsc	front post single crochet(s)
FPtrc	front post triple crochet(s)
gm(s)	gram(s)
hdc	half double crochet(s)
lp(s)	loop(s)
oz	ounce(s)
patt	pattern
PC(s)	popcorn(s)
prev	previous
rem	remain(ing)
rep	repeat(ing)
rnd(s)	round(s)
sc	single crochet(s)
sk	skip
sl	slip
sl st(s)	slip stitch(es)
sp(s)	space(s)
st(s)	stitch(es)
tog	together
trc	triple crochet(s)
yd(s)	yard(s)
YO	yarn over

* An asterisk (or double asterisks **) is used to mark the beginning of a portion of instructions to be worked more than once; thus, "rep from * twice more" means after working the instructions once, repeat the instructions following the asterisk twice more (3 times in all).

† The dagger (or double daggers ††) identifies a portion of instructions that will be repeated again later in the same row or round.

— The number after a long dash at the end of a row or round indicates the number of stitches you should have when the row or round has been completed. The long dash can also be used to indicate a completed stitch such as a decrease, a shell, or a cluster.

( ) Parentheses are used to enclose instructions which should be worked the exact number of times specified immediately following the parentheses, such as "(2 sc in next dc, sc in next dc) twice." They are also used to set off and clarify a group of stitches that are to be worked all into the same space or stitch, such as "(2 dc, ch 1, 2 dc) in corner sp."

[ ] Brackets and ( ) parentheses are used to provide additional information to clarify instructions.

Join - join with a sl st unless otherwise specified.

The patterns in this book are written using United States terminology. Terms which have different English equivalents are noted below.

United States	English
single crochet (sc)	double crochet (dc)
half double crochet (hdc)	half treble (htr)
double crochet (dc)	treble (tr)
triple crochet (trc)	double treble (dtr)
double triple crochet (dtrc)	triple treble (trtr)
skip (sk)	miss
slip stitch (sl st)	slip stitch (ss) or "single crochet"
gauge	tension
yarn over (YO)	yarn over hook (YOH)

An Important Word about Gauge

A correct stitch gauge is very important. Please take the time to work a stitch gauge swatch about 4" x 4". Measure the swatch. If the number of stitches and rows are fewer than indicated under "Gauge" in the pattern, your hook is too large. Try another swatch with a smaller size hook. If the number of stitches and rows are more than indicated under "Gauge" in the pattern, your hook is too small. Try another swatch with a larger size hook.

Filet Review

Filet Crochet is a combination of chains, double crochets, single crochets and slip stitches.

These stitches form a series of blocks, some open, some filled (see **Photo A**). The blocks then form beautiful designs.

Our filet afghan is worked from a chart of blocks (squares). On the chart, each vertical line represents one dc and each short horizontal line represents a ch-2. A block with a black dot is a filled block.

Photo A

Open Blocks
An open block is formed by a double crochet, a ch-2 and a double crochet (see **Photo B**).

On the chart, a row of open blocks looks like this (**Fig 1**).

Photo B

Fig 1
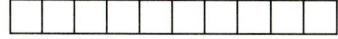

It is worked as follows:
 dc in next st, ch 2, sk next 2 sts of prev row, dc in next st

At the beginning of a row, the first dc and the first ch-2 of an open block is formed by a turning ch-5 that is made at the end of the previous row. At the end of a row, the last dc is worked into the 3rd ch of the turning ch-5.

Filled Blocks
A filled block is formed by four double crochets (see **Photo C**).

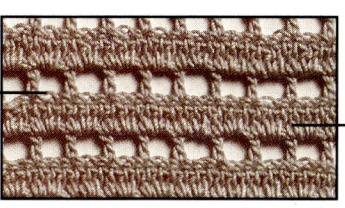
Photo C

If the filled block is over an open block, it is worked as follows:
 dc in next st, 2 dc in next ch-2 sp of prev row; dc in next dc

Note: Double crochets can be worked into the chains of the ch-2 sp, if desired.

On this chart, a row of filled blocks is over a row of open blocks (**Fig 2**).

Fig 2

If the filled block is over another filled block, it is worked as follows:
 dc in each dc (see **Photo D**).

On this chart, a row of filled blocks is over another row of filled blocks (**Fig 3**).

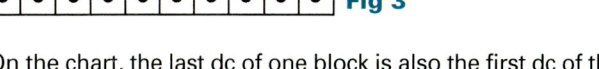
Fig 3

Photo D — Filled Blocks Over Filled Blocks

On the chart, the last dc of one block is also the first dc of the following block.

Working From a Chart
When working from a chart remember that for each odd-numbered row (right side of work), you work the chart from right to left; but for each even-numbered row (wrong side of work), you work the chart from left to right.

Fringe

Basic instructions
Cut a piece of cardboard half as long as specified in instructions for strands plus ½" for trimming allowance. Wind yarn loosely and evenly lengthwise around cardboard. When card is filled, cut yarn across one end. Do this several times, then begin fringing; you can wind additional strands as you need them.

Single Knot Fringe
Hold specified number of strands for one knot of fringe together, then fold in half. Hold afghan with right side facing you. Use crochet hook to draw folded end through space or stitch from right to wrong side (**Figs 1** and **2**), pull loose ends through folded section (**Fig 3**) and draw knot up firmly (**Fig 4**). Space knots as indicated in pattern instructions.

Double Knot Fringe
Begin by working Single Knot Fringe completely across one end of afghan. With right side facing you and working from left to right, take half the strands of one knot and half the strands in the knot next to it, and knot them together (**Fig 5**).

Triple Knot Fringe
First work Double Knot Fringe. Then working again on the right side from left to right, tie third row of knots as in **Fig 6**.

Fig 1	Fig 2	Fig 3	Fig 4	Fig 5	Fig 6
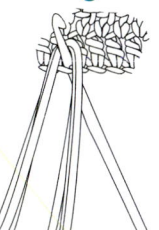	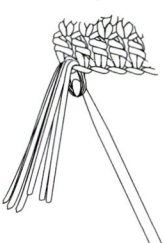			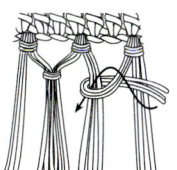	

General Information

Stitch Guide

Chain - ch: YO, draw through lp on hook.

Single Crochet - sc: Insert hook in st, YO and draw through, YO and draw through both lps on hook.

Half Double Crochet - hdc: YO, insert hook in st, YO, draw through, YO and draw through all 3 lps on hook.

Double Crochet - dc: YO, insert hook in st, YO, draw through, (YO and draw through 2 lps on hook) twice.

Triple Crochet - trc: YO twice, insert hook in st, YO, draw through, (YO and draw through 2 lps on hook) 3 times.

Slip Stitch - sl st:
(a) Used for Joinings Insert hook in indicated st, YO and draw through st and lp on hook.

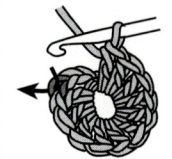

(b) Used for Moving Yarn Over Insert hook in st, YO draw through st and lp on hook.

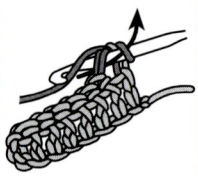

Front Loop - FL: The front loop is the loop toward you at the top of the stitch.
Back Loop - BL: The back loop is the loop away from you at the top of the stitch.
Post: The post is the vertical part of the stitch.

Overcast Stitch is worked loosely to join crochet pieces.

Metric Charts

INCHES INTO MILLIMETERS & CENTIMETERS (Rounded off slightly)

inches	mm	cm	inches	cm	inches	cm	inches	cm
1/8	3		5	12.5	21	53.5	38	96.5
1/4	6		5 1/2	14	22	56	39	99
3/8	10	1	6	15	23	58.5	40	101.5
1/2	13	1.3	7	18	24	61	41	104
5/8	15	1.5	8	20.5	25	63.5	42	106.5
3/4	20	2	9	23	26	66	43	109
7/8	22	2.2	10	25.5	27	68.5	44	112
1	25	2.5	11	28	28	71	45	114.5
1 1/4	32	3.2	12	30.5	29	73.5	46	117
1 1/2	38	3.8	13	33	30	76	47	119.5
1 3/4	45	4.5	14	35.5	31	79	48	122
2	50	5	15	38	32	81.5	49	124.5
2 1/2	65	6.5	16	40.5	33	84	50	127
3	75	7.5	17	43	34	86.5		
3 1/2	90	9	18	46	35	89		
4	100	10	19	48.5	36	91.5		
4 1/2	115	11.5	20	51	37	94		

mm - millimeter   cm - centimeter

CROCHET HOOKS CONVERSION CHART

U.S.	1/B	2/C	3/D	4/E	5/F	6/G	8/H	9/I	10/J	10 1/2/K	N
Continental-mm	2.25	2.75	3.25	3.5	3.75	4.25	5	5.5	6	6.5	9.0